The Shell Book of
GOLF

The Shell Book of
GOLF

Peter Alliss

David & Charles
Newton Abbot   London   North Pomfret (Vt)

Shell U.K. Limited, while sponsoring this book, would point out that the author is expressing his own views.

British Library Cataloguing in Publication Data

Alliss, Peter
  The Shell Book of Golf
  1. Golf
  I. Title
  796.352   GV965

  ISBN 0-7153-7988-7

Library of Congress Catalog Card Number: 81-65956

Typeset by Typesetters (Birmingham) Limited
and printed in Great Britain
by The Alden Press, Oxford
for David & Charles (Publishers) Limited
Brunel House Newton Abbot Devon

Published in the United States of America
by David & Charles Inc
North Pomfret Vermont 05053 USA

Contents

Introduction

This book is the result of 40 years spent in and around the game of golf. I cannot remember a time when the game did not dominate my life.

My father Percy, himself a famous golfer who might well have won the Open on not a few occasions, was for many years the club professional at Ferndown in Dorset and it was there that I absorbed enough of the rudiments of the game to become a good scratch player by my mid-teens. It was from there that I first set forth into the wider golfing world of, first, local alliance competition and then, in the late 1940s, my first entries in full professional tournaments and the Open itself followed.

Later, with my brother Alec, I moved to Parkstone where I stayed 13 years and, with a very tidy 63, still hold the course record. My next berth was in Yorkshire, at Moor Allerton, a formidable Robert Trent Jones course, where I stayed until 1980 and then came a move to Surrey, and the opening of Old Thorns Golf & Country Club. Old Thorns Golf & Country Club is *ours*, that is Alliss Thomas Golf Construction Ltd, along with Pat Dawson and Ken Wood of 'mixer' fame. So now I have the course opening in '82 and London nearby for work etc.

Although I was a club professional throughout the 1950s and 1960s, it was then the world of tournament golf that claimed most of my attention. During this period I won more than 20 major tournaments but for me the highlights remain playing for Great Britain in the Ryder Cup and for England 10 times in the World Cup.

My memories of courses come not so much from memories of 'a good day out', as they do for most golfers, but as the scenes of tournaments won and lost, Ryder Cup triumphs and failures.

The serious days of my competitive career are over, but golf is as important to my life now as ever because of my involvement in TV golf programmes, writing, and my business partnership.

Peter Alliss, 1981

1
Playing

Two approaches

There are two ways to move something: you can either pull it or push it. This applies equally to swinging a golf club and over the years golfers have discussed at great length which is the better of the two methods. Some argue that the left hand and arm should dominate and sweep the ball away, while others say it is a right-handed game and you should 'throw' the clubhead into the ball. In this book, to save words, I will have to talk as if all golfers stand right-handed to the ball. Even the top teachers approach the game differently. The important thing is to know how you personally hit the ball and to adopt a set-up suited to your style.

There are two types of swing to consider: the first is known as the 'modern swing' and the second as the 'classical swing'. In my view many of the best teachers of the game live in America where the professionals avail themselves of excellent instruction material put out by the PGA of America. In the early 1970s they produced a PGA study programme called *Methods of Teaching* and for many in the business it is still the Bible and focuses on some superb players from past and present such as Tony Lema, Byron Nelson, Ben Hogan, Jack Nicklaus, Arnold Palmer, Tommy Bolt, Gary Player, Bobby Jones and the old-time British champions.

The study programme requires teachers to observe whether a golfer predominantly pulls the club into the ball, or throws it. Obviously not every swing can be placed clearly in one or other group, but broadly this is the distinction.

Teachers who advocate the pulling concept consider it to be best for our modern-day equipment. Those who teach the old-fashioned classical swing point to the champions of the past who used it with such success. It would be foolish to present one method of playing golf as the best one and I want to go into the whole subject of striking the ball at length and try to examine

7

(left) Harold Hilton, Open champion in 1892 and 1897, completes his backswing. Note that he has 'let go' of the club; *(right)* one of my favourite golfers, Bobby Locke, playing at the peak of his career at Worthing in the 1950 Spalding tournament. Look at that turn, club well across the line (*Bert Neale*)

the thinking behind, for instance, the different methods of Harry Vardon, Nelson, Hogan, Trevino, Nicklaus, Watson and others.

After developing a fine game, even the champions sometimes reach greatness because of a vital hint or thought, which for them, unlocks some problem. Perhaps the supreme example of this is Hogan who reached greatness late on in his golfing life after years of combat with the dreaded hook when he learned to produce a far more reliable fade. No two players are alike but, like Hogan, at their own level, they can come to understand the basic principles of a good method suited to them.

Five-times British amateur champion Michael Bonallack used to say he liked to concentrate on one gimmick, one thought or idea. It might be to look at the back of the ball, or to try keeping the left heel down in a wind. A week later he'd throw the idea out and try something else. Before the 1921 Open, English amateur Roger Wethered was given a tip by Harold Hilton and for the next fifty years he kept this helpful advice in his mind. Hilton had merely suggested that Mr Wethered, well over 6 feet tall, should stand a little 'open' (that is, with the left foot and hip withdrawn a couple of inches or so from the swing line) to the ball as this would help him clear his body. 'I followed his advice and tied the Open', said Mr Wethered; on television I was delighted to hear Lee Trevino giving the same advice as Hilton had. However, when cross-questioned about advice from other famous players, Mr Wethered was the first to admit that Harry Vardon had advocated a closed stance, as did Hogan, Locke, Nelson and many others, while a majority of leading players today stand a little open. Why is it, then, that so many fine competitors have been able to achieve grand results with differing approaches? We shall see.

Long hitting

A golf ball hit hard and long gives enormous satisfaction. Arnold Palmer swayed about on the follow-through from the impetus of his powerful forearms and hands, while Bobby Jones was always balanced. His length came from rhythmic acceleration and exact striking. Cyril Tolley, pipe in mouth, was one of the longest hitters in the 1920s and 1930s and another British amateur, Joe Carr, took over in the post-war years. And can you remember Jack Nicklaus peeling off his sweater and thumping one through the last green in the play-off for the 1970 Open at St Andrews? And how about the poise and power of that final drive by Tony Jacklin up the 18th to victory at Royal Lytham in 1969?

Jack Nicklaus derives much of his big hitting from powerful thighs, but not many of us could copy him. I've watched Ben Hogan driving and been totally spellbound. There have been dozens of excellent big hitters — think of Roberto de Vicenzo, Leopoldo Ruiz and the superb striker, Henry Cotton. The list could go on. What have they in common, and can we learn their ancient and modern secrets?

Byron Nelson achieved something in the game without equal, winning eleven tournaments in a row in America just after World War II. He always spoke about the uniformity of the swing and insisted that we use the same swing for every shot, with minor alterations to stance according to the differing lengths of shaft used. He was quite emphatic on this and said he was completely unaware of making any attempt to swing even a driver differently from a wedge.

For driving Byron Nelson addressed the ball with a closed stance, which is what Ben Hogan advocated for powerful hitting, but it was not, as we shall see, what Harry Vardon thought. With Nelson everything, apart from his closed stance, was squared to the line of flight. Hips, shoulders, chest,

(*left*) The characteristic finish of a Palmer drive, brought about by the powerful thrust of the right hand and arm through the hitting area and beyond (*Peter Dazeley Photography*); (*right*) Edward Blackwell, who like Nicklaus drove the last green at St Andrews — but with a gutty. Good points to note are the very full shoulder turn and the high position of the hands; more doubtful are his loose grip with the right hand, too much foot movement and overlong backswing

were all in line to the flagstick. You will notice in pictures of Nelson that he gripped the shaft of the club so that there was about an inch of it 'unused'. This is interesting, for Nelson was a tall man, well over 6 feet tall, and you would have expected him to have used the full length of the club. I believe he went down the shaft for extra control.

Nelson peaked immediately after World War II but was very much the modern golfer as far as his method was concerned. He took the driver back a long way before he let the wrists bend. The great players seem to do this to achieve the maximum arc of swing, essential if you are going to give the ball a good hit. 'At no time', said Nelson, 'should you make a conscious effort to cock the wrists.' In the 1980s this has become basic to the methods of nearly all the modern masters. The club goes back from the ball in 'one piece', by which I mean that to the observer it is taken back by hands, arms and shoulders, with the wrist break not coming until the backswing nears completion. Although a few of today's stars reverse this process and break the wrists early I believe that the average golfer is much better off with the Nelson method, for it encourages a full shoulder turn and pivot while the early wrist break means that there must be a tendency to merely lift the club up and back with the hands and be satisfied with little coiling of the back and shoulders.

At the top of Nelson's swing the sole of the clubhead pointed directly at the target, with left shoulder underneath the chin. Coming down, he said he felt his left hip and shoulder were pulling the club down, leaving him ready to unsnap his hands in the hitting area. He said he had the sensation of the right hand trying to catch up the left and talked of releasing hand power. He accelerated into the ball and at the upright finish of his swing, in total balance, the shoulders had effected virtually a full revolution from the position they had been at the top of the backswing.

Three other Americans have most influenced modern thought about striking a golf ball: Bobby Jones showed how good balance, rhythm and timing, from a narrow (feet quite close together) stance, could tame the shortcomings of the hickory shaft and his game will always be described as classical. Then there came Ben Hogan, and Nicklaus. Hogan was a light man of only medium height and hit the ball with a whiplash action, gaining maximum distance from a shut stance and hands that tore into the ball. On the backswing his wrists started to break only as he reached waist height and pictures of him in this position look as though he is pulling a rope in a tug-of-war!

For years Hogan battled against a hook and in his youth took the club back so far you felt sure he could see it at the top from his left eye. He shortened his swing, got the left wrist a little under the shaft together with other adjustments he later described in his instruction book *The Modern Fundamentals of Golf*, beat his hook and became an awesome player, respected by everyone and even referred to as 'Mr Hogan', one of the highest honours in America and not even accorded to Jack Nicklaus.

Some professionals of his day thought Hogan might have done more to pass on his knowledge to younger players, and to give away his secrets, but I don't think he had a secret and I agree with Sam Snead, who said Hogan simply learned to hit the golf ball with his full power without hooking the thing out of sight. Once he mastered that he had the iron will and determination to beat any player in the world at that time. And, as Hogan once said to Jones, that is all any champion can do.

Driving the ball is of vital importance and there are numerous examples to examine. Did you know, for instance, that the great Nicklaus suggests you stand up straight to drive? He uses an interlocking grip, swings the club

high with right elbow away from the body and crashes it down, into and through the ball, taking advantage of tree-like thighs to help pull everything else through. And those of you who, when trying to hit a particularly long one, heave the club backwards might heed the Nicklaus advice. In these circumstances he takes the club back more slowly and with more shoulder turn.

Nicklaus really 'thinks' his way round the course, plotting hazards and pacing off yards to the centre of the green. He doesn't guess distances with the eye as they did in the old days, and he tries to hit his teeshots to exact fairway positions. If there is trouble on the left side of the fairway, he drives the ball from the left side of the tee. This enables him to aim towards the right side of the fairway, away from the trouble.

If the wind is left to right, Nicklaus tees his ball on the left of the tee and tries to let the shot swing with the wind for as many yards as possible. Compared with other great players, he tees the ball up fairly high and, like a good boxer, hits his weight — sometimes, particularly in the 1960s, sending the ball well over 300 yards and arousing disbelief even in Bobby Jones, a fair hitter himself.

Driving methods have evolved over the years, but I think the club player is best helped copying stars of the past who hit the ball in a much less fierce and athletic way. After all, you cannot expect a desk-bound businessman to hit it like Palmer!

Harry Vardon was the man who created the traditional grip on the club and the way he held his hands is copied today by almost all the world's top-flight players. Vardon had definite views on how to drive a ball and said the club should be drawn into the backswing rather more slowly than you intend to bring it down again. Slowly back, he argued, is a maxim both wise and old. The club should begin to gain speed when the upward swing is about half made, and the increase should be gradual until the top of the swing is reached, but never so fast that control of the clubhead is lost.

Vardon said the head of the club should be taken back fairly straight from the ball for the first six inches along a line he used to mark out on the turf. After that, a tendency to sweep it round the body should be avoided; the club should be kept close to the straight line going back until half way up.

Possibly Vardon was ahead of his time in regard to instruction. He maintained that the old St Andrews style of driving made for an undesirable sweep round the body going back and argued that his method was easier and produced better results. This carrying of the head of the club upwards and

(*opposite*) All a man can do is beat the best golfers of his day and Bobby Jones did just that in 13 major championships before retiring at the age of 28 in 1930

Jack Nicklaus (*Peter Dazeley Photo-graphy*)

backwards seemed simple, capable of explanation in a few shots, or words.

It is interesting at this stage to compare Vardon with another great driver of the ball, Sam Snead. He advocated a similar takeaway and film of Snead shows the club going straight back for a long way. With Snead, the wrists began to cock very late and he emphasised that the wrists have no power, being merely hinges. Snead thought it essential the clubhead be swung in a consistent path and that the wrists remain in a position that helps to keep the left arm straight. The right elbow should be close to the body, added Sam.

Vardon was unquestionably the father of modern golf thinking. Even Walter Hagen was spellbound by Vardon in the 1913 US Open and watched him practise lofted iron shots from a downhill lie. He faded every one of them and the groove of his swing was so obvious, Hagen said, you could almost see it. Said Hagen: 'I was so impressed that during the last round when my swing started to leave me, I imitated Vardon's and it worked, too. Fact is, I almost caught him with his own swing.'

If there is a golf secret, it was Vardon who pinpointed it. He said the head must be kept perfectly motionless from the time of the address until the ball had been sent on its way. The least deviation from this could mean disaster, he added, and when a drive has been badly foozled, the most usual explanation is that the eye has been taken off the ball. It is a wise piece of advice to tell golfers to keep their eye on the ball, but it is really the *head* that must be still. Vardon maintained that only one drive in a hundred is missed because the eye is not on the ball; it was the moving of the head that caused failure. Until the ball has gone, the head must be kept still and he wrote that it should not be moved by as much as a sixteenth of an inch, adding that he realised this was not really possible with humans! In fact even the best golfers *do* move their heads on the backswing and some, Nicklaus most emphatically, compensate for this by turning the head to the right before they begin the backward movement of the club. There is then no sudden jerk of the head that is the thing most to be avoided.

When the head is kept still and the club has reached the top of the swing, the eyes should be looking over the middle of the left shoulder. Most players, he said, fall into every evil trap the spirits set for them and tend to lift their heads away from the ball during the upward swing. This is what is often imagined to be taking the eye off the ball and, when carried to excess, the eye, struggling to do its duty, finds difficulty in keeping sight of the ball over the left shoulder and sometimes, for an instant, loses sight of it. An examination of photographs of Vardon at the top of his swing shows there is very little margin for moving the head if the ball is to remain in full view throughout the swing.

(*left*) A relaxed address position: Jerry Pate, 1976 US Open champion (*Peter Dazeley Photography*); (*right*) Harry Vardon at the turn of the century. Note the relaxed position but achieved by what would be thought of as 'errors' today: bent left arm, up on the left toe, excessive hip turn — and the hands are by no means high

He also thought that during the upward swing, the right shoulder should be raised gradually. From the moment when the club is first taken back, the left wrist should begin to turn the face of the club from the ball. When this is properly done, said Vardon, the toe of the club will point to the sky.

This turning or twisting process continues all the way until at the top of the swing, the toe of the club is pointing downwards to the ground. When the wrist has not been working in this way, the toe of the club at the top of the swing will still be pointing upwards. Vardon always suggested that a pupil should stop at the top of his swing, release the right hand, and have a good look at where the clubhead points and where the clubface points. This is a vital point but a different method of teaching to some advice given in later years by professionals who were 'shut' at the top — and often hooked wildly as a result.

Vardon maintained that during the backswing the arms should be gradually 'let out' and spread well away from the body, and early photos of the great man showed just what he meant. He found it much easier to pose for pictures in the 'how to do it' section than for pictures of 'how not to do it' that book publishers were so fond of in past years.

In the upward movement of the club, the body should pivot from the waist alone, maintained Vardon, and there must be no swaying, not even to the extent of one inch! When the player sways, the stroke he makes is a body stroke pure and simple. The body is trying to do the work the arms should do, and in these circumstances it is impossible to get as much power into the stroke as when it is properly made.

Vardon was convinced, and said so in his book, *The Complete Golfer*, that great emphasis should be placed on getting the backswing just right and if this were achieved, then much less attention need be paid to the downswing even though it is the vital part of the swing.

His advice concerning the top of the swing is interesting. Some teachers advocate a pause here but Vardon said we should be careful not to dwell. The club has been gaining speed right up to the top and though in theory there was a pause of some kind when the turning point was reached, it was only 'an infinite part of a second' and the golfer, he thought, should scarcely be conscious of it. He must obviously avoid a sudden jerk, but if he dwells at the top his upward swing, even with all its perfection and training, all will have been wasted and he will be hitting the ball with the disadvantages of a golfer who had merely placed his swing in a backswing position to begin with, and had tried to generate a rhythmic hit from there.

So Vardon was emphatic that we get the backswing right, don't hang about at the top, and let the clubhead gain speed gradually downwards until it makes solid contact with the ball, at which point the clubhead should be travelling at its greatest speed. The entire movement must have rhythm and smoothness, with no semblance of a snatch, a jump or a double swing.

Vardon warned golfers not to let the clubhead escape from its proper path coming down into the ball because, when this happened, a player by instinct would try to save the stroke with some compensatory action and, if he threw the club on to the outside path and drew it across the ball, he would slice. He recommended that both elbows should almost graze the body coming down.

Vardon had a delightful turn of phrase. He threatened his pupils by saying any kind of sway would probably allow out the old enemies of the slice and the pull, and they would mock the golfer with a grin and make him a most unhappy fellow!

Like other famous golfers, Vardon said the movement of the feet and legs is important. In addressing the ball you stand with both feet flat and firmly placed on the ground, the weight evenly divided between them, and the legs so slightly bent at the knee joints as to make the bending scarcely noticeable.

This position should be maintained during the upward movement of the club until the arms begin to pull at the body. The easiest and most natural thing to do then is to raise the heel of the left foot and begin the pivot on the left toe and this allows the arms to proceed with their uplifting process without hindrance.

Do not ostentatiously pivot on the left toe because you think it right, said Vardon, but let it happen naturally and then only sufficiently to allow you to reach the full extent of the swing without difficulty. While all this is happening, the weight of the body is gradually thrown on to the right leg, which accordingly stiffens until the top of the swing when it is quite rigid, the left leg being at the same time in a state of freedom in that it is slightly bent towards the right, with only enough pressure on the toe to keep it in position.

Vardon's teaching should never be forgotten; to the man who has never driven well, he said, the whole process might appear tedious. 'All these things to attend to, sir,' he might say, 'and only a second in which to do it!' It indicates, he said, just how much there is to this wonderful game, more than any of us suspect or shall ever discover. He argued that the upward swing is everything: if it is bad or faulty, then the downward swing will be wrong and the ball will not fly with conviction. If the backswing is perfect, then the prospect of a good hit is indeed splendid.

It is a lovely expression — to 'hold the wrists firmly' — and Vardon seemed to think that when this was achieved they would take care of themselves. But he said there was a tendency, particularly when the two-V grip is used, to allow the right hand to take charge of affairs as the ball is struck, and the result is that the right wrist, as the swing is completed, gradually gets on top of the shaft instead of remaining in its proper place. The result of all this is a pulled ball. When this fault gets out of hand, the clubhead suddenly turns over and the ball, crippled, is done for and struggles along only a few yards like an injured bird! Vardon said he found the ladies often suffered from this plague and the remedy seems to be that if the club is taken back in the Vardon way, it will have a greater chance of coming down correctly.

Vardon had an idea which he claimed added distance. He said that with the direction and force of the swing your chest is turned round until it faces the flagstick. There is an art in timing this movement. If it takes place a mite too soon, the Vardon stroke is ruined; if too late, it is ineffectual. When made at the right time it adds valuable yards. Photos show that Vardon's body was indeed thrown forward with every ounce. He was like a good prizefighter, hitting his weight.

When a golfer slices, Vardon said, he may be standing too near the ball

Full shoulder turn, restricted hip turn from Andy Bean and Ray Floyd (*Peter Dazeley Photography*)

and the clubhead may be drawn across the line. Standing too near could mean the clubhead being taken back outside the line Vardon recommended.

The fine art of curing slicing and hooking has advanced over the years, of course. British teacher John Jacobs always says the flight of a golf ball provides most answers, while Nicklaus admits that a swing takes place so rapidly that it is often impossible to detect the key mistake that causes a bad stroke. But Nicklaus thinks we should all look for clues, and one thing to look for is the divot mark and the direction it takes. The most obvious is when the divot slants to the left of the target. This means a golfer has swung across the ball and the result will seldom be an accurate shot; a slice is almost inevitable. A divot cutting into the turf in the direction right of the target could mean a push to the right, or a hook if the clubface is shut. The clubface in both these instances is imparting spin usually unwanted, unless the golfer is trying to fly the ball round an obstruction such as a tree.

20

Nicklaus says that if the divot is straight, but the ball starts to the right and flies even further to the right, the ball has been hit with an open face and the hands have probably got ahead of the stroke. It all sounds simple enough when reading an instruction book, and it really is straightforward. It took a long time for golfers to delve into the mysteries of the game and actually learn about it. The printed word has always helped in any form of education and golf is no exception.

Before returning to the teachings of Vardon, let me quote another modern player, Neil Coles, who has won £200,000 in Britain and Europe, much of it before the really huge prizes came along. Neil thinks that just as the accomplished marksman goes through a routine of check and doublecheck before he pulls the trigger, and as the pilot goes through a routine to ensure everything is set to go before taking off in an aircraft, so a golfer must go through the basics of stance and grip. He should establish beyond any doubt exactly what it is he is trying to do. He should see the flight and shape of the shot before he hits it.

Vardon stressed that the head should be kept motionless and the body pivoted easily at the waist; but when the club is half-way down, the left hip is allowed to go forward a little — a preliminary to, and preparation for, the forward movement of the body soon to begin. The Vardon weight is being gradually moved back again from the right leg to the left. At the moment of impact both feet are equally weighted and are flat on the ground, just as they were at the address.

This interesting point has been stressed by several top-line golfers over the years. They saw the impact position as the same as when they stood to the ball before starting back but Sam Snead thought that, up to impact, he was shoving power into the ball with the right leg, and that the right shoulder had dropped just a little.

And there were other slight differences. Vardon usually played golf in a jacket claiming it helped to hold the swing together, while the more athletic Snead did not. The American used the full length of the shaft to drive while, in photos anyway, Vardon gripped down the shaft and had less of Snead's supple coiling action. The ordinary golfer probably has a much better chance of swinging like Vardon than Snead. After impact Vardon said his weight was thrown on to his left leg, which stiffened while the right toe pivoted and the knee bent just as its partner did in the earlier stages of the stroke.

The wrists were often mentioned by Vardon. He wrote that they should be held tightly and there should be little play in them. He didn't believe the long shots came from the wrists and even went on record as saying there is no pure wrist shot in golf. Those who try to play wristy shots are likely to

remain high-handicap players all their lives. Though even here there are many exceptions. Watch Isao Aoki hit every shot from full drive to putt or Christy O'Connor, Charlie Ward and myself. All the time the wristiness.

James Braid, another very tall golfer of distinction, and one of the 'Great Triumvirate' — Vardon and Taylor were the other members of the threesome — was quite emphatic about one thing, writing before World War I. He did not recommend the way Harry Vardon stood at the address, feeling that such a position 'invited the body to come into the shot too soon'. Instead he liked players to stand square and had a great deal to say on the subject of body twist.

In order to hit a long drive, Braid instructed pupils at Walton Heath in his later days to stand well back from the ball and eliminate all stiffness from the body. He advocated a full and free body turn.

Photos of Braid driving the ball showed him, in jacket, with his back to the target at the top of the swing, with quite a bend in the left arm and with a stance which, for the life of me, looks more open than square. Maybe it was a case of 'do as I say and not as I do'! Indeed, before the days of high-speed photography, even the greatest of golfers were in error when they described what they *thought* they did in their swings. Just as the movie camera showed us that the horse never has all four hooves off the ground, it has taught us a thing or two about the golf swing — that the backswing and downswing do not follow the same path, for instance.

Braid taught the use of all the elasticity in the human frame, fully stretched and employed in making a drive. Like Vardon, he didn't think much of the advice to take the club back slowly. He frequently told people to get plenty of speed through the ball. He liked a suspicion of a bend in the right knee at address because he took the view this gave a feeling of comfort, suppleness and power. At the top of the swing this right leg, he said, should be stiff and rigid. This is part of the preparation of what he called 'momentary high tension' at the top, in anticipation of a quick reaction.

Braid thought the left wrist, going back, should gradually turn so that at the top of the swing it would be right underneath the shaft, the toe of the club having thus been brought to point 'turfwards'. In later years Reg Whitcombe, winner of the 1938 Open at Sandwich, said this was quite wrong and that the club should be taken back naturally with no attempt to heave the left wrist under. But more of this later. It was argued by Braid that he wanted a state of tension at the top. Of course, Braid was using wooden-shafted clubs.

(*opposite*) Two champions: John Henry Taylor, five times winner of the Open and W. G. Grace (right), the great cricketer, at Westward Ho!, Taylor's home club

No other golfer has 'lasted' as long as Sam Snead (*Peter Dazeley Photography*)

Old Braid, long since dead, was more than 6 feet tall and although he called most men 'Sir' and touched his cap, I believe many golfers were frightened of him. He could bellow in his Scottish accent and sent shivers down the spines of many a young professional. But he was wise, and much respected.

He knew why so many club golfers fail to improve at the game as fast as they would like. 'They do not practise sufficiently,' he said. 'Now then, this may appear a simple thing to say but I must point out that most club golfers do not practise at all.' Maybe James Braid was right. Is this true today? Arnold Palmer of America was quoted as saying even British professionals didn't practise much in the 1960s — but added they were charming people nonetheless!

Braid said the most club golfers do is putt on the practice green near the clubhouse. And they have an excellent one at Walton Heath, where he was based for years. Braid noticed the members there used to have a delightful programme in the old days. They would play all day, 36 holes, and because they teed off without much more than a daisy-cutting practice swing, dear old Mr Braid said they had forgotten what they were doing last time round and had little confidence in consequence of that. You can almost hear him say it!

Our Mr Braid noticed that in the old days, when a man came up to the club looking for a game, he didn't always find one. Nobody about to make up a four. So what happened? The golfer did not play at all, but returned home after a drink, or a look at the magazines. What he should have done was to practise alone, with one club; that, said Braid, is the way to improve. And he might have added that it would have been a good idea if 'Sir' had taken out one of the young assistants who might have taught him a thing or two. And, if the member was really lucky, he might have had a playing lesson with Mr Braid himself — and that wouldn't have done him much harm, I'll wager!

Sam Snead, whose career has run from the mid-1930s and may not yet be over, obviously knows what he is doing: he has won tournaments and shot sub-par rounds when well into his 60s — by far the longest career at the top. So smooth was his swing that one golf writer said he was the Rolls-Royce of players.

Snead reckoned balance to be the beginning of any golf shot. He turned the toes outwards, had his arms swinging freely and said the ball and hands were practically in the same vertical plane. He drove from a slightly open stance, unlike old James Braid. The Snead knees were loose at address.

Movie shots were taken of Snead as he drove, and they were shot from the target so this straw-hatted American was shown hitting the ball into camera. At his peak Snead drove the ball as far as Nicklaus and turned his back on the target at the top of the swing — a terrific pivot. The left heel was well off the ground. An athletic man, Snead was double-jointed and appeared to hit firmly into a solid left side. Unlike James Braid, Snead maintained it is hard to keep your balance if you reach for the ball and he thought that when you drive you should stand erect; photos show him almost doing this, except for a slight bend forward from the waist.

He was a strong man, with powerful hands, yet he always said a golfer should only grip a club about as tightly as he gripped a hammer. He considered it most unlikely anyone would let go of the grip during a swing.

Snead had a delightful West Virginian accent and an easy-going attitude to golf. He was unhurried, rather like Bobby Locke, and had a fine rhythm. He claimed a golfer should enjoy a few waggles before easing into the backswing and that the whole thing should flow without any kind of jerk. The left arm, he said, should be held straight, the arm an extension of the clubshaft. In this he differed from the older players, who often bent their left arm quite considerably either because of restrictive clothing, or because they did not have the Snead elasticity.

Nothing about the Snead swing suggested that anything was tightening up, although at the top of the swing he was coiled for the smash downwards into the ball. Snead's secret, if there was one, was that he was able to swing at the ball as so many golfers swing at a daisy. He said we should all take it easily and lazily because the golf ball isn't going to run away while we're swinging. Or as Johnny Miller put it when, for a year or two, golf was a very easy game, 'Make yourself like jelly and just slop the club through the ball.'

In other words 'hurry absolutely nothing about the swing', said Sam. The only speed involved was the clubhead through the ball and there he really let rip but retained his poise, never hurling himself about like such later players as Arnold Palmer and Gary Player, who attacked in a more dramatic way.

It is peculiar then that Snead was never able to win his own US Open title, although he won the British once, and the Masters and US PGA three times each, and all the other big championships. But Americans regard their Open as the big one and his failure to win must be put down to temperament. On one occasion in 1939 Snead needed a par 5 to win and a 6 to tie. He took 8 and was never allowed to forget it. Several years later he had another excellent chance but a missed putt on the last green meant failure again.

Golfers have walked thousands of miles after Sam Snead with one thing in mind. They wanted to steal his secret and many young professionals certainly learned a thing or two. But if you could have got Sam alone to talk about golf, he might have given away two valuable tips free of charge!

Sam told once how to cure a slice. He said spin is the factor that causes a ball to swerve and maybe that seems obvious. He said a hook is caused by the ball being hit from inside the line of flight, an in-to-out swing as we call it; the slice comes about by hitting across the line. Well, most of us know this.

Snead said those who slice try to cure themselves by yanking the clubhead away towards the left-hand side of the fairway. The more they yank, the more the clubhead came across the ball. His answer: let the clubhead fly out to the right-hand side of the fairway if you want to beat the slice. In other words, re-route the follow-through and don't drag the club across the ball to give it that awful slicing spin. Line of swing is all important. And the hook? Snead reckoned he'd overdone the in-to-out movement and should try to hit the ball to the left-hand side of the fairway. 'Too simple', do I hear you say?

However, while this is excellent stuff, it may well be that you hook or slice for other reasons: a weak grip, incorrect stance, or bad swing line, for instance. My advice is to talk it over with your local pro.

Others who followed Snead to steal secrets watched his easy walk, which seemed to match the pace of his swing — he never darted about like Dai Rees, whose swing was as fast as any present-day player except perhaps Dale Hayes. In sudden-death play-offs Snead was a demon and beat the mighty Hogan more than once. He was unflappable and would never play until he was good and ready — except those times when he 'blew' the US Open.

Easy-going Snead used to talk about flinging the club into the ball and on the follow-through would keep the right arm extended as far as it would go. Whatever he did on the course was worth copying, which is why they all followed him.

Fitness for golf is not often mentioned, except notably by Gary Player. But looking back into writing of the 1930s I see that Reg Whitcombe, winner of the 1938 British Open title, emphasised the importance of good chest expansion for plenty of fresh air, a firm abdominal wall and an erect, supple spine.

Whitcombe was a friend of my father Percy, and both men contributed to the story of golf. My father was an excellent player and had an enormous following. Whitcombe was the more controversial in teaching and in action. He told people to 'breathe' their way to a better game, said they weren't fit and had theories about deep breathing before you drove, as well as exercises in the office and while walking between shots. He suggested pulling in the stomach muscles and heaving in great gulps of fresh air. He told golfers to sleep with the windows open and to empty the lungs after a night's sleep by having a good yawn, with plenty of stretching.

On the game itself, Whitcombe warned that golfers should not place the left thumb on top of the shaft. He let it run down the side of the leather as he claimed this produced no stiffening of the muscles. Whitcombe produced a wonderful little book called *Golf's No Mystery* and in it suggested pupils learn to hit the ball one-handed, alternating hands — this, of course, on the practice ground.

The Whitcombe method was different. He said golf is a right-handed game and should be played in a natural manner, as natural as a kid whacking a conker with a walking stick. He wouldn't hit the conker away from himself, left-handed. He'd sock it with the right. This big-handed man warned against over-doing the straight left arm as it induced tension — I would have enjoyed watching him give a lesson to Gary Player!

We cannot leave Whitcombe and the drive without recalling exactly what he had to say about getting the wrists under the shaft at the top of the swing. He urged us to banish this thought because with the wrists there, he said, we should slice every shot.

Reg Whitcombe thought every club should be swung with what he called a bread-and-butter swing. You just stood further away for the longer shots and, in the case of the driver, you found out how far away to stand by dropping the shaft to the left knee to measure the distance.

He altered his stance slightly for the shorter clubs, making it more open. He explained that with a driver you must not tilt the face towards the ground. The face must come to the ball either square to the target or just moving upwards, away from the ground.

He thought the 2-wood gave club golfers more trouble than any other club. Some pros advise leaving this club in the bag, or not even buying one. However Mr Whitcombe knew the answer and explained the way to play the club with some obvious logic. He said we should notice the metal plate on the sole. It was there for reasons other than decoration. It protects the club when it is thumped down into the ball — and that is the secret of success with the brassie. Thump down and make contact with the ground half an inch behind the ball, and don't mess about! The same or similar principle to the sand-iron shot.

Apart from his grip, Whitcombe had one other peculiarity. He addressed his driver two inches behind the ball. Another greater golfer, Jack Nicklaus, does not ground his driver at address, which just shows that we all have our little eccentric ways, and long may this be so.

Not all the great players of the past told us how high to tee the ball. It's important. Whitcombe said tee it up one inch, while Doug Sanders has been known to use extra-long tee pegs, to encourage hitting on the upswing. Others said tee it low to slice and tee it high to hook. Most reckon you should place the ball just inside the left heel to drive, and move it back progressively towards mid-stance for the more lofted clubs.

The Americans continue to publish potted guides which tell, among other things, how to drive the ball further. Big hitters have special techniques they apply whenever they want to generate more power. One of them is to grip the club in a strong position with the left thumb on the right side of the shaft at about 2 o'clock. Hold tight throughout the swing with the last three fingers of the left hand. The guide also advises us to adopt a closed stance with the feet wider apart than usual and to address the ball more forward, or opposite the left toe. Extend the left arm going back and keep the head behind the ball.

It is also recommended to make a full and deliberate shoulder turn. Move the left shoulder under the chin and coil the body muscles. Great power is generated from the body muscles.

On the downswing turn the body as fast as possible. Keep it moving and start with the hips, following with the shoulders, then arms and hands. Uncock the wrists as late as possible in a whip-cracking action. Let the clubhead follow the flight of the ball and finish with the hands high.

Other sure-fire tips include trying to strike the ball on the upswing with your drive — don't top it! Try slanting the toe forward when teeing the ball, strike the ball on the lettering because this is supposed to avoid the hidden seam in the ball. And — wait for it — exhale on the downswing!

All this may make you hook (or commit Hari Kari!). If so, open the stance slightly, allow the left hand to dominate the swing, don't roll the wrists, use an upright swing, finish with the hands above the head.

Well that was the advice in 1968, along with a whisky commercial. They gave it away free! 'No wonder', perhaps you'll say.

By now you should have some idea how to drive a ball. Simply speaking, there are several ways but a group of Americans, including Snead, Ken Venturi and Gene Sarazen, produced a potted version and beginning with the backswing, it went something like this:

1 Start the swing in one piece, hands, arms and shoulders together after a slight forward press.
2 Turn left shoulder under the chin and pivot in one flowing movement. Start the clubhead low along the ground. Swing the clubhead slowly but rhythmically, setting an even tempo.
3 Don't cock the wrists at the start and don't pick up the clubhead. The right knee should be firm, slightly flexed. The left knee should bend in

towards the right. Lift the left heel only slightly and roll the left foot on to the instep. The right foot should be dug firmly into the ground and the left arm should be straight, but not rigid.

4 Swaying must be avoided, the head steady and the eyes should be looking at the back of the ball. Break the wrists as the clubhead passes the horizontal, with the right arm at this point relaxed and the elbow down. The palm of the right hand should be pointing upwards. The booklet suggested that at the top of the swing we should pause.

5 The downswing should be convincing and determined. (Oh, I like that.) It should be started with the left arm and left side and the weight should be shifted. Keep the left side firm and the left arm straight. Delay uncocking of the wrists and think of driving the butt end of the grip into the ground as you start down. Whip the clubhead through from the inside line with both hands, throwing the clubhead towards the target and away from the body in a single flowing action.

6 Finally, follow-through as long as possible towards the target and extend the left arm as far forward as possible. This helps to keep the clubface on target for a fraction longer. Finish with hands high, facing hole.

Summary

I think you'll find that all this is good advice. Also I like the suggestion to stalk up to the ball from behind, choosing the line.

At this point I'd like to try to sum up varied thoughts on the overall swing. Put simply, the purpose of the all-out driving swing is to bring the clubhead squarely on the intended flight path and through the ball at the maximum possible speed.

I remember well how my particular American friend Tony Lema, sadly killed in an aircraft accident, addressed the ball. His left arm and the clubshaft were in a straight line down to the ball. His knees were flexed slightly and he bent forward from the waist. The way he won the Open at St Andrews in 1964 was a joy to see.

The set-up and alignment have always been regarded as vital in golf. If these are wrong, a player must compensate during the swing. His brain will tell him to do this, but it is an unnecessary complication and something to be avoided. You see, alignment with the target will predetermine how the body will be used in the swing. For instance, when a golfer lines up to the right of the target as Bobby Locke used to do, it meant he had to give it an 'over-the-top' action with the upper body moving fast to bring the ball back. When the set-up is directly to the target, no compensation is needed and a golfer can pull the clubhead straight through the ball with his left side.

What I'm saying is that we shouldn't complicate the golf swing. All right, the left foot at address is pointed out slightly, while the right foot is at right angles to the intended line of flight. With the top players the hips tend to be slightly open while the shoulders and knees remain square. And of course the left shoulder and hip are higher than the right because of the way you are obliged to hold the club. But these things are basic and looked so natural with stars like Lema. Grip pressure is in the last three fingers of the left hand and the left thumb — whatever Reg Whitcombe said in the old days — is on top of the shaft with the back of the left hand facing the hole.

Try to drive the ball using the simple methods; they've been tested and proved. In a hundred years someone may have further improved the method, but we shall not be around to see.

The Alliss method

When I was learning my golf as a small boy at Ferndown I can remember my father saying, 'Golf can be as simple or as complicated as you care to make it'. He was a great believer in simplicity in golf, and the game to him was not one of great difficulty but it had to incorporate simple rhythm and balance.

I have always tried to follow my father's simple ideas on the game as I am convinced that if you are fortunate enough to be able to play golf with a clear and simple outlook, in many ways you have a tremendous advantage over some of the others who find even the most straightforward shot a major production.

Let me give you what I consider to be the basic principles of the game.

For the good players, and remember that it is always much simpler to teach good players than beginners, I would like to pass on a series of ideas and tips and thoughts, gimmicks if you like, that have stood me in very good stead over the years. For the beginners I hope that, by following some of these reasonably simple thoughts, you, too, will be able to knock two or three shots off your handicap. Get as many things right as possible *before* you swing.

Grip
First we start with the grip. It is essential to get a good, sensible, solid grip of the club. Personally I do not care whether you use the double-handed grip (in which all the fingers of the right hand grip the club), as used by Dai Rees, the interlocking grip (in which the fore-finger of the left hand fits between the little finger and the third finger of the right hand, producing

(opposite) Royal County Down — the short 7th (*Bert Neale*)

32

(*above*) Sunningdale — the clubhouse and oak tree by the 18th green on the Old Course (*Bert Neale*); (*below*) Royal Lytham & St Annes — looking across the 16th and 17th fairway towards the clubhouse (*Bert Neale*)

the effect of locking the two hands together) as used by the great Whitcombe brothers and latterly by Jack Nicklaus, or the more popular Vardon grip, where the little finger of the right hand hooks over the index finger of the left. What I am convinced is essential is that the two hands *must* work together. Golf is a two-handed game and one can become too conscious of trying to play with either one hand or the other, so remember that the club is gripped with two hands, working as one unit.

I am also a great believer in getting the club well in the fingers of both hands, triggering the right fore-finger well down the shaft.

Once you have got a sound grip with which you can control the club throughout the entire swing, and is good enough to retain its position even *after* the ball has been struck, you must then build a stance. Leave no gaps between the fingers for the right forefinger, which acts like a trigger.

Stance
As we have seen there are three basic stances: open, shut, closed. I have always believed that you should place your feet when standing to the ball the way you put them down when you walk, so that if you are a five-to-one, 'ten-to-two', pigeon-toed or even a Charlie Chaplin 'quarter-to-three' walker, it must be easier for you to stand to the ball in that way.

If you are a 'ten-to-two' man, it is difficult to turn your toes in and lock the hips, for remember that once you turn one foot against the other you get resistance in the hips and shoulders and you are beginning to defeat your first idea of rhythm and balance.

Distance from the ball is also very important, but more important still is to keep your hands up at the address position. Do not stick your head down in your shoulders like a tortoise and bend your back down to the ball. Bend down from the waist slightly with the knees flexed, keeping the back fairly *straight* and the arms reaching out to the ball. If you drop your hands you put a kink in the chain and it is possible to hit the ground anywhere within a radius of two feet of the ball. The wrists too high can make your swing 'uncomfortable'.

Ball position
Once you have your good grip and sound stance, the next important thing is a constant ball position. I have always been a great believer in trying to keep the ball in the same place pretty well for every shot, and that is just inside the left heel.

Of course, with a driver the length of shaft takes you further away from the ball, and as the shafts get progressively shorter you get nearer to the ball and bring your right foot in towards the left. Although the ball looks to be

(*opposite, top*) Dai Rees: all fingers of the right hand are on the shaft. A good grip for the ladies or if, like many handicap golfers, you do not have strong hands; (*opposite, bottom*) A good view of the Vardon grip — note the huge hands; (*above*) Ben Hogan: left thumb down the shaft and the back of the hand leads towards the target, right fore-finger acting as a trigger (*Bert Neale*)

(*above, left*) Percy Alliss demonstrating an open stance in the 1930s for a fairway wood. For added control he has 'gone down the shaft' a couple of inches; (*right*) There's plenty wrong with this set-up but Fuzzy Zoeller is a recent US Masters champion. His posture is very stooped, hands low and very close to the body giving a considerable 'kink' in the chain (*Peter Dazeley Photography*); (*below, left*) Peter Thomson believes in a constant ball position — just inside the left heel (*Sidney Harris*)

in the middle of the feet it is, in fact, still in its original position just inside the left heel.

Now you have your good grip, sound stance, ball position, head up giving yourself plenty of room to swing the arms free from the body. Everything else should be 50/50: weight, leg flex, grip pressure — and look at the ball with both eyes.

The drive

We will start with the driver now. I have had great success by teeing the ball high and also teeing the ball low, and this is just one of my first ideas that may help you again. If you have a lot of trouble on the left-hand side of the fairway, tee the ball low because invariably with a driver (there being little loft) the ball will cut if you keep the hands ahead of the clubhead so if you tee the ball down you have almost the same effect as playing the driver off the fairway, and most people find it very difficult to hook a ball from the fairway with a driver because of its lack of loft.

If you have trouble on the right-hand side of the fairway, tee the ball higher and force yourself to aim down the right-hand side of the fairway. Put the ball forward, even ahead of the left toe.

Make sure you swing freely back slightly inside the line of flight, or just normally with a good pivot. Make sure you have really good shoulder turn, keep your eye on the ball and hit past the chin. You should get a nice medium-flying ball with a little draw on it. Release the clubhead and remember a 2- or 3-wood is easier to use.

For beginners the most difficult clubs to play are the longest and least lofted ones. Most people are frightened of a driver and 2- and 3-irons. A difference between beginners and top pros is that beginners tend to aim more and more to the left of the target; while professionals tend to aim more and more to the right of the target.

When going through a reasonably lean spell and not hitting the ball well, it is amazing how one of your chums usually says, 'Well, of course, you are aiming well to the right of the green. Bring the ball forward. Aim it left. Aim at the left-hand side. Let the ball come in.' So hit away from, not round yourself.

Even the top pros find it hard to believe that they have got into this way of playing, so it is quite understandable for the beginner who is aiming a good thirty or forty yards left of the target with the ball well outside his left foot and, of course, slicing away merrily, to find it hard to believe that he is, in fact, lined up correctly when it must feel to him as if he is aiming seventy or eighty yards right of the green.

One of the main problems of driving for the average golfer is, as I have mentioned earlier, slicing. This can be caused by incorrect ball position, lack of pivot, lifting the arms, chopping down and across the ball, no pivot in the backswing or opening the left shoulder too quickly in the through swing.

So once you have got your good grip, good stance, good ball position, make the swing as wide as you possibly can when using your driver. Don't be frightened of letting the arms go right back.

I see my own swing as a straight line but, of course, many players see their swing as a curve. A very good example of this is Dai Rees who swings *round* — whereas I swing *up*.

Other players see shots differently, everything from a putt to a drive. I know two very good putters. One can see it 'left half of the hole' and one can see it 'right half of the hole' when it will probably be a dead straight putt, but they just have it in their own mind that they must aim it left half or right half; they both putt very successfully.

It is the same with longer shots. Bobby Locke always saw shots coming in

This must have been a good shot: Henry Cotton driving at Moor Park in 1937 is perfectly balanced (*Sport & General*)

(*left*) For Bobby Locke every shot was a draw. Here he is in 1950 (*Bert Neale*); (*right*) Ben Hogan at Wentworth in the Canada Cup in 1956. His swing is markedly flat. If they tell you at the club that you are swinging flat say 'Yes, I'm trying to get it into the Hogan position' (*Bert Neale*)

right to left. Ben Hogan, in his best years, played with a view of the ball coming in from left to right.

Suppose we are working on the concept of hitting the shot straight from *A* to *B*, rather like firing a rifle or throwing a cricket ball. I think only in a forward direction. I believe that people who throw — playing darts if you like or throwing a cricket ball — are not worried about how they take their arm back; they are looking at the target and the brain is sending its messages to the hand to throw the object forward to that target.

That is why I try to get as many things right before I start my actual swing. (This idea also covers clubs to suit your size, length, weight, required grip thickness.) I do not think it is possible to change one's mind successfully in mid-swing. The more things you get right before you start, the more chance you have of hitting the ball correctly, provided, of course, you still follow the original basic ideas of throwing such as keeping the body reasonably still, watching the ball, balance, etc.

Another tip that has helped me tremendously with my driving at different periods is gripping down the shaft, so that the length of the club becomes

41

the same as 4-wood or even a 1-iron. But here again one must make a decisive sweeping hit at the ball.

For normal driving on a fairly open course, the old saying of the great American Tony Penna 'tee it high and let if fly' is probably very true, because if your set-up is right and you look at the ball and swing well through, invariably you get the full weight of the club behind the ball — and away it goes.

I have rather likened my own particular swing to a windmill, the actual body of the windmill being my body and the arms of the windmill being my arms, which can turn and control the club.

I have never been a lateral mover such as Peter Thomson, Ben Hogan, Joe Carr and Fred Daly. I sometimes wish I had, because they seemed able to hit the ball so late that their worst shots were usually 'thin' ones that went forward towards the target doing no great damage.

My body rotates as in a cylinder with the arms outside the top of the

Harry Weetman (*Bert Neale*)

cylinder swinging independently. This is the whole key to golf — you have two entirely separate movements, the body rotating one way and the arms swinging another. So if there is any one 'secret' it lies in controlling these two different movements.

The secret of golf, besides trying to get a swing that repeats as often as possible, is to bring the club face back to the ball square enough to hit the ball through to the target. If the club is turned in, of course, it will go one way. If it is open it will go another. So you must concentrate on the club coming back to the ball square to the line of flight. Once you synchronise these two movements, then you have a good golf shot, and the man who synchronises it most often is invariably the best player.

Remember there are so many ways of playing golf well. I need only remind you of Bobby Locke, Harry Bradshaw, Harry Weetman, Ed Furgol, Arnold Palmer, Jack Nicklaus, Gary Player and Byron Nelson. They all have different swings, different grips, different set-ups to the ball, yet basically the main principle is the same — good rhythm. If you took pictures of each of them within two feet either side of the hitting area, from the waist down only, it would probably be very difficult to tell one from the other.

So do not be put off if you have an unusual swing. It is up to you to get it to repeat. All these other people have been able to do it, but remember again they have worked for hours and hours at their game and practised hard. You cannot do it by sitting in the office from Monday to Friday, rushing out to the course on Saturday morning, paying your money to enter the monthly medal competition and being very disappointed if your first drive does not go 230 yards straight down the middle of the fairway. Everybody could play golf well, or better, if they were prepared to put a little more time into it, and a little bit more effort into their practising, though if you do, and win, you may well be branded a 'pot hunter'.

Fairway woods

As far as the fairway woods are concerned I think I employ the same basic principles as for the driver: sweep the ball away.

Now there are many good wooden-club players who take considerable divots from the fairway. I am thinking or Peter Thomson, Arnold Palmer, and sometimes even Gary Player, but here again I have found it easier to try to sweep the ball away than to hit down on it like an iron.

Remember also that a 4-wood properly hit, especially with the modern 4-woods which have reasonably deep faces, would only probably be ten to twenty yards behind a good hit with a 2-wood.

43

If you go down the shaft of a 4-wood you can generate a little bit more clubhead speed and hit it absolutely 100 per cent flush, as I remember I did in the 1965 Ryder Cup matches at Birkdale, where I played probably the finest 4-wood shot of my life when Christy O'Connor and I were partners in the four-ball match against Arnold Palmer and Dave Marr.

It was on the 18th hole and I really felt, on that occasion, that the 18th hole was out of reach for me in two. But I stood up on the fairway and aimed it down the right-hand side of the course as I was going through a period of (a mental picture again) drawing the ball. I went down the shaft about half an inch and really caught it right on the button and drew it in about fifteen yards; it ran up about eight or ten feet from the hole.

This you can do with your fairway woods by thinking of keeping the swing wide, staying over the ball, keeping and using your height, a good firm grip, squeezing with the fingers. Try to take the tension out of the arms and flex the knees. Use both hands and do not be frightened of letting the club sweep through to the target. Watch the ball as long as you possibly can. Remember the old saying of 'hit past the chin'. Keep your height and for the first 18 inches take the club back smoothly — if you do this you will be a much better player.

Returning to the backswing, I again emphasise the simple basics. Once you can play, you have a backswing. Once you have learned to take the club back correctly, everything else follows on.

Henry Cotton's thoughts on the importance of the hands are very important, and he is correct in pointing to the advantage that professionals have because they play every day and this gives them strong hands. So you must train your hands to be strong. There are various exercises you can try but squeezing a squash ball in the pocket or pushing the fingers of each hand hard against each other will do very well.

Legs and knees play a tremendous part in the golf swing. If you get yourself set and draw the club back with the arms, the mere fact that you are taking it back away from the ball and your legs are firm but relaxed with the hips well opened will ensure that the club will go back in a straight line.

Remember that many people tend to over-swing. You can generate tremendous clubhead speed from a three-quarter swing if the club travels the right path, so do not be too worried about getting the club back past the horizontal, like a Crenshaw or Watson. Very often in a long backswing, especially in the case of a handicap golfer, the last foot or so of clubhead movement results from the hands letting the club drop. No greater power results from this. Perhaps less, because the hands have to lift the club up again rather than hitting down directly towards the ball. However, do not stray too far in the other direction and swing too short. It used to work for

Ben Crenshaw at impact (*Peter Dazeley Photography*)

Doug Sanders, about whom they used to say that he could swing a golf club in a telephone box, but the club golfer with a short backswing is liable to heave with his body to compensate for the fact that he has not given his arms a chance for it is the distance you get your *hands*, not the clubhead, away from the ball that counts for power. Then, let the club go. Hit through the ball. Keep the body still. Just think of the arms generating power and

Severiano Ballesteros really lets the club
go through (*Peter Dazeley Photography*)

hitting the ball with the clubhead. A ball has always to be hit with the clubhead, not with your shoulders, not with your knees, not with your left ear!

These, then, are my basic principles for the wooden clubs.

Between drive and green

I hope you don't believe that piece of nonsense that 'you drive for show and putt for dough'. The teeshot is arguably the most important shot in golf, which is why so much space is devoted to it in this book. But now we've walked down the fairway to play the second shot and provided the ball is in a good position, the excitement and the possibilities of a birdie obviously mount.

The golf swing is beautiful when executed with balance and accuracy. In the early 1920s the art of swinging at a golf ball was disclosed by the ultra-rapid camera and for the first time golfers could see what they were really doing. And this produced some red faces, because although teachers had said this and that, they suddenly saw they did not always practise what they preached. The camera could not lie. Or could it?

Very similar positions at impact from Lanny Wadkins and Hale Irwin (*Peter Dazeley Photography*)

The bent left arm of Harry Vardon and once again we can see he has swung well past the horizontal and is up on the left toe. The right leg forms a rigid 'post' around which he swings

For two shillings you could buy the complete swing sequence of Gene Sarazen in a hardback book published by the Photochrom Company of London and Tunbridge Wells. It showed thirty-six positions of Sarazen's iron shots from the fairway, taken when he was playing at his very best. They showed that Sarazen pointed the shoulder at the ball at the top of a short controlled swing, that his left arm wasn't absolutely straight, that his left heel came from the ground. In fact it showed everything golfers wanted to see and study. In my view it helped clear away many myths and possibly assisted the ordinary golfer to become better so that now, deluged by instruction, the weekender hits the ball with more skill and understanding than he did before the camera froze the action.

But pictures cannot convey the full feel of the shot. How do you hit down into the turf in order to make the ball go upwards? The only real way is to get out there and practise and play. Once the pictures started to 'move' with books that could be 'flicked' to see the action, however, instruction had a useful new dimension.

Pictures showed that experienced golfers employed the same kind of swing with their driver as they did with their long irons. True, they made minor adjustments like standing more open and nearer the ball for the short shots, and with the pitch shots they sometimes went right down the grip and maybe picked up the club more sharply. But the basic swing was the same.

As long ago as 1907 some of the champions of the day posed for George Beldam. They each hit twenty shots and he produced what was called a cinematographoid which gave reasonable results.

Beldam warned that only the expert could interpret what the camera showed and never gave up the hope of eventually finding the key that would make the lessons clear to all. Thinking about golf in those days was confused. One writer suggested one method, one another and some of the top players had no clear idea of how they hit the ball. But the filming went on, and at considerable expense in those days.

Certainly the camera pictures helped to define the principles common to all top players and showed how the champions produced a movement which led onlookers to feel the maximum effect had been achieved with the minimum effort, a good gauge for everyone during practice.

'Let the weight of the club do it', said the old professionals and gradually they discovered that the art of good golf lies in a uniform increase in the speed of the clubhead. Ernest Jones, not to be confused with Bobby Jones, used to demonstrate this by tying his penknife to a handkerchief or piece of string and letting it swing, showing that the maximum speed of the weight was achieved at the exact position a golf ball would be resting.

Royal Birkdale — the short 7th hole (*Bert Neale*)

(*above*) Killarney — the 13th green of this beautiful course on the shores of Loch Leane (*Bert Neale*); (*below*) Gleneagles — the 14th green on the King's Course (*Bert Neale*)

The principle common to many of the champions is that the motive power comes from within the body and is transmitted outwards to the club. The hands are the medium through which this power acts, but they do not supply the motive power. This, anyway, was the conclusion of the early golfing 'movie-makers'.

However, we have already discussed the woods; you are now placed on the fairway ready to hit your next stroke to the green. Let's assume you are faced with the dreaded long iron; being told by experts that 2- and 3-iron shots are easy must be one of the most annoying things in a handicap golfer's life. In fact they are hard, very hard.

Many of our top professionals prefer to use a 4-iron or even 5-wood to the straight-faced iron. Why is this? The answer is quite simple. The less loft a club has the more difficult the shot is to control. Hence the 1- and 2-irons and driver are, without doubt, the most difficult clubs in the bag.

It would be so easy to tell you to drive with a 2-wood (after all Bobby Locke and Peter Thomson both won Open Championships during the 1950s driving with lofted woods) or to buy a 5-wood to do the work of the No 2 and 3 irons, but if you wish to continue your own self-made hell by persevering with the long irons, I will endeavour to help you.

I have tended to be a 'sweeper' rather than a big divot taker — very important with the long irons. If the club face is at all closed at impact the ball will never get airborne. Position the ball opposite the left heel, stance slightly open, hips and shoulders pointing slightly left of target, knees bent but firm. Head up — always remember to keep the head up at the address; do not tuck it in like that tortoise I mentioned earlier.

Also try to remember there are no *really* straight lines in a golf swing. Perhaps for a split second the left arm appears rigid and straight at the top of the backswing, and the same impression may be had at impact but, in the words of the immortal Harry Vardon, 'I love to play against a man with a straight left arm'.

At the address position keep the weight evenly distributed, if anything more on the balls of the feet than the heels.

Break the wrist fairly early in the backswing, but remember to keep the first nine inches of the backswing slow and easy. After that you can accelerate as much as you like as long as you build up the rhythm and speed gradually. Try to maintain the same pressure of grip throughout the swing. Do not regrip or tense up, especially at impact — this is a fatal error and can lead only to disaster.

A three-quarter backswing is all that is required, the left heel to be kept near if not on the ground when you have reached the top of the backswing. This, of course, is much easier for tall people, but I think many handicap golfers tend to swing about on their feet too much. You should have the feeling in the backswing that your hands are travelling up or breaking *up*, not *round* the body.

From the top of the backswing the first movement I feel is the opening of the left hip and the pulling down of the hands, and my last thoughts are making sure I hit the ball with the clubhead. My right hand acts as a second clubface, throwing the head at the ball, and at the same time keeping me behind the shot.

Once again I should like to stress the importance of the arms and hands. After you have acquired a solid stance, all you really need to worry about is getting your hands and arms to work back and through the ball, keeping the head and body as still as possible.

A slight lateral movement is acceptable as long as it is controlled as in the cases of Hogan, Thomson, Fred Daly or Joe Carr, but the reverse of this, a dip on to the left foot carrying ninety per cent of the weight, is fatal. Why? Because you cannot hit the ball from that position without tilting back again onto the right foot before impact, thereby striking inches behind the ball.

The shorter the iron the simpler the swing should be. The shaft is shorter and therefore easier to control. From the 6-iron down to the wedge, you should concentrate on accuracy and not length. The feet are a little closer together, ball still well forward, bringing your right foot in towards the left with knees flexed. And remember you can square either the bottom of the blade, or the top, to the target. If you line up with the top it will look as if you are closing the clubface, like Neil Coles; if the bottom, the club will look open. It is the path through the ball that counts. Again, use a three-quarter backswing with the arms and hands controlling the whole movement.

Remember your distribution of weight for these shots is a little more on the left than the right. A little more divot may be taken at impact, because the shorter shaft will make your swing steeper, but again may I stress the point of thinking in a *forward direction*. Do *not* let your swing peter out at the ball. Let the arms take the club to a good, full follow-through.

Remember the points I have already mentioned: grip, and stance and ball position. Get these right before you start — once your swing is under way it is too late to do much about it.

Pitching and chipping

Let's suppose you missed the green with your approach shot, and are left with a short pitch or a little chip shot. Rolling three shots into two is the name of the game.

There are golfers who have been quite outstanding at the short game. Bobby Locke, Bob Charles, Bob Rosburg and many others reduced the game at times to what we call 'scrambling'. Don't turn your nose up — it doesn't matter how you get the ball into the hole. It's how many, not how. When you watch golf on TV notice how consistently and apparently confidently Tom Watson gets these little shots close to the hole. Indeed, perhaps I am wrong in speaking of turning three shots into two. Watson and Ballesteros are two players that come to mind as attempting to hole out with their twenty to forty yard little pitches and chips.

The short game is about all shots within a hundred yards of the pin. These are the accuracy shots and do not call for great strength or power, and it does not matter whether you put the ball close to the flag with a 4-iron or a sand iron. Some golfers may have a favourite club; others use just about everything in the bag. The only test is how near the pin you get the ball.

The great mistake I find amongst high-handicap golfers is that they underestimate the fact that they are playing with a round object with a tendency to roll. Perhaps it is because they have read about the low-flying wedge shots of our American colleagues that pitch on the green by the hole and never move more than two or three feet in either direction. This, of course, is true when playing the big ball on to well watered, banked-up greens but the majority of times these are not the conditions under which we play. Remember also that these golfers hit much harder and with more precision: these factors add up to much more backspin.

The first thing I advise is to visualise the carry and then the run because, to me, all these shots are in fact a sort of pitch and run. My interpretation of a pitch shot is one that does not move more than four or five feet once it has hit the green.

Many years ago I was considered to be rather suspect from one hundred or so yards of the green, but I was very fortunate in playing a lot of golf with Ken Bousfield, one of the great exponents of the short game. Ken believed in rhythm and a slow, relatively long swing, but I am the first to agree that this does not suit everybody and I have said many times before there are too many ways of playing golf well. This is the method that I followed and it suited me well.

Let us start first of all with the shot from a hundred yards short of the green — from the fairway. I think it is important to get a good look at the shot in hand — whether the pin is on the front of the green or the back, whether there are bunkers in the way, whether there are hazards at the back of the green, front of the green or whatever. So many people just stand up and hit the ball towards the green and hope that it is going to finish somewhere near. This is no good. Make up your mind and satisfy yourself where the flag is and the type of shot you are going to play.

I always try to pitch my ball round about the front of the green; I have discovered that it is much better to pitch the ball on to the actual putting surface every time than bumble it up short and hope for a good kick towards the flag.

On a shot of a hundred yards, when you use a pitching club, remember that under normal conditions the ball will roll from five to ten yards.

One of the best tips ever passed on to me was to liken all these shortish shots to playing bowls or lobbing a cricket ball. You must get a mental picture of the ball rolling towards the hole or the target.

The stroke is played almost entirely with the arms; with knees bent, throw the arms through to the target. When you move in closer, say to within fifty yards, the same rules still apply. You see the target; you see the problem before you; you then slot in your mental picture of what you are trying to do and promptly do it.

Always try to think in a forward direction, never a backward one, and remember at all times that the ball will roll.

For the chip shots from just off the edge of the green, I imagine that my right hand is the club face and I only extend my right arm to the club face, pick up the ball in that right hand and throw it under arm towards the flag.

If you stand on the edge of any green and just play bowls with half-a-dozen gold balls I think you will be surprised how quickly you can start rolling them to within a few feet of the hole, but as soon as you use a club you may top or fluff them. Remember to let the ball work for you. What does it matter if you take a putter, a No 2 iron or a wedge? Bobby Locke always used his wedge from the very edge of the green and many of today's top players seem to favour the sand iron most of all. It could not suit all people but no one can deny the mastery of these players. For you, practice with a 6, 7, 8 or 9 iron may be the answer but try to be confident and proficient with at least one club.

Sand

Many players fear bunker shots and I assume it will take them more than one shot to get out. Yet the sand shot is really quite easy, if you only take the trouble to understand the basics. It is rather like playing ducks-and-drakes except that, instead of skimming the flat stone across the water, you are using the broad-soled flange, or base, of the modern sandblaster.

It was not always this way. Old-time players used sharp-edged lofted irons to extract themselves from trouble and the skill involved was much greater

(*above*) A bunker to be feared. Not a few competitors found themselves in this one at Royal St George's, Sandwich, in the 1981 Open (*Peter Dazeley Photography*); (*right*) Harry Vardon using a sharp-edged niblick. Note how far he has gone down the shaft and the 'texture' of the sand!

than that required for today's stroke that is almost bought with the club. I remember J. H. Taylor describing how his nerves were badly on edge as he stepped into a bunker at a Prestwick Open, playing in front of thousands of excited Scots. For some reason he did not strike the ball properly, and it fell back into the sand. He was shattered and maintains that this single shot cost him the Open Championship, because it demoralised him. Every golfer knows exactly how this sort of thing can happen.

Getting out of sand can be achieved with a putter, a chip, a pitch, a full iron hit a little 'thin', or an explosion shot — the blast. Now and again you even see the ambitious taking their 4-wood and, quite often, succeeding.

Most of the teachers say we should swing the club back on the outside of the arc when in sand. The feet have been planted firmly, not only to secure a firm footing, but also to lower the body in order to help the process of hitting beneath the ball and in effect to tee up sand on which the ball rests until it is almost lifted out. The reason the experts choose to swing at the ball from the outside of the line is to inflict a slapping or spanking action which gets the ball up quickly and helps it land 'flat' on the green.

When you get into a bunker, the quick simple answer is to get the ball out and don't try anything too fancy. There is more than one way of playing sand shots of course. If the ball is buried, or in a heel mark, methods other than the explosion shot should be disregarded. In fact the buried ball, according to 1951 Open Champion Max Faulkner, comes out best when you turn the blade inwards, almost hooding it at address. This enables the blade to dig down and under the ball, and also prevents the blade being deflected away from the target.

Former US Masters winner Doug Ford, in the 1950s, was a spectacular sand player. He had been told by Lloyd Mangrum that the actual club he was using was ill-suited to sand shots and promptly bought another one. With that club he almost made the ball talk and he said he would rather be in a greenside bunker, lying well, than faced with a huge putt, maybe over wicked burrows and bumps.

Ford, like Gary Player, reckons a golfer must understand sand before he really knows how to play the shots. Seaside sand, fine and silky, is very much more simple, he says, than blasting out of inland 'dirt' sand. The mental side is important too. When you are in sand it is mainly because you misjudged the previous shot. In other words it's your fault. Forget about an unlucky bounce. You put it there. Now get it out.

The basic sand shot should be hit from an open stance, says Ford, and the ball positioned slightly inside the left heel. The open stance also causes the clubhead to move outside its normal path on the backswing and the object is to slice across the ball.

The result of cutting a ball out of sand is that it will drop on to the green with right-hand spin and should curl away quite sharply. Because of this Ford always aimed his trap shots to the left of target to allow for the break. He claimed you should use little body action — just sufficient to give you rhythm. The swing is mostly with the hands, arms and wrists and the head remains absolutely steady.

The Ford bunker shot was not directed at hitting the ball, but at a point behind it. In other words he, too, was hitting the sand about one inch behind it. If it was not a long shot, then experience told Ford to shorten the backswing because less power was required. At impact he felt he was flicking the ball, but the shot was completed with a follow-through at least as long as the backswing.

What I like about the Ford advice concerned the sand types. Assuming the ball to be sitting reasonably on sand he would hit three-quarters of an inch behind it in coastal sand, and with the blade reasonably square. For 'dirt' sand he would hit one inch behind and with the blade more open, and if the ball had sunk a little into loose sand, he would hit two inches behind it with the blade hooded.

Uphill lies in the sand are the hardest because the clubhead encounters more sand as it sinks in. The ball must be played well forward in the stance and you have to swing harder and concentrate on the full follow-through. A deep penetration of the sand is not wanted, so keep the blade open. On a downhill sand-shot, Ford hooded the blade and played the ball further back in the stance, with the clubhead going in two inches behind.

Without a shadow of a doubt, the good old sand bunker took its biggest beating when Gene Sarazen came to Britain in 1932 and won the Open Championship. He attributed his success not just to his obvious ability, but also to a brand-new club, the sand wedge, which he had designed to bounce the ball out of traps. Previously a poor sand player, he had worked the previous winter on producing a broad-soled club that would float through the sand, adding and subtracting lead until he was satisfied with the results. They included both British and US Opens in the same year.

This new-fangled club took the skill from the shot. It was so clever that even the average player could make it work. The flange at the base of the club was so thick that the club could not sink without trace and even the duffer could escape.

Sarazen told everyone that the swing you used with this club was much the same as with any other escape shot. Basic changes in the address were made to allow for a more cutting shot, but the club did the work for you. Hurry folks, to your nearest pro shop and buy this new wonder club. And they did!

Neil Coles explodes to the first green at Walton Heath during the PGA Match-Play Championship in 1965 (*Sport & General*)

Sarazen suggested the player dig his feet in to establish a firm base. This meant the player became a little lower in relation to the ball and made it easier to go down the grip a little. The whole approach developed confidence. Open the clubface, said Sarazen, set your hands slightly ahead and take the club away smoothly. Then, with the cutting shot, simply blast the ball out, lifting out a whole section of sand with the ball. The ball rose up the bunker face dropped softly on to the green.

Old-timers said it was almost cheating. But overnight the fear and dread of the bunker had been removed — well, almost. But for a moment, let us assume that you are not a wizard in sand and go over what Sarazen had in mind, assuming that you have the correct club for the job because in this instance it is no use manufacturing the shot with a lofted iron. You must have a sand wedge.

Over the years Gary Player has gained a fine reputation for his bunker play. His fame was not earned without a lot of hard work and practice from sand traps and George Blumberg, who helped him on his way, used to tell how Gary would spend hours in sand, not just flopping them out, but trying to hole them.

Knowing how a ball will react from a bunker shot, according to its lie and the type of sand it rests in, is the first step in beating the problem, maintained Gary. He realised that some high-handicap golfers regard the whole business of sand traps with horror and if you were lucky enough to have a bunker lesson from this great master, you would find confidence.

Gary Player talks about 'reading the sand'. It is rather like reading the green. You have to weigh everything up and having played golf round the world, he has probably experienced every type of sand known to man — and knowing how the grains affect the club and the ball is an important part of any expert's technique. Wet bunkers require a different technique from those that boast fine, silky sand and although you cannot get down and feel the sand with your hands before you play the shot, there is nothing in the rules that says you cannot test the surface with your feet.

Gary reckons the best bunker players he has seen are Julius Boros and Sam Snead. They both play the shot with a slow, flowing action and maintain a lazy rhythm throughout. If you can achieve rhythm and are getting a regular flight pattern, with the ball kicking to the right as it hits the green, then you are probably ready to add a touch of finesse to your sand play. I would add the little Australian von Nida to this group.

Player maintained that from deep powdery sand your club digs in fairly deep and, because a large cushion of sand will be formed between the clubface and ball, the ball will pop up more quickly with a steeper flight. Because of this, you will have to give the shot a little extra. From wet sand you'll get more backspin, so once again give it enough energy to get you up to the flagstick, even if it means pitching past the pin to allow the ball to spin back.

All this sounds simple enough. But Gary never shirked from telling eager listeners in his clinics that sometimes they might put their shots into bunkers which had little sand in them. Player says that in these circumstances we should forget the sand iron and use instead a pitching wedge or 8 or 9 iron and play the shot almost as a normal pitch shot. He admits that it is not an easy shot and suggests you practise it!

Other awkward shots to be discussed occur when your ball has fallen into soft sand from a height. It is then that the ball, half buried, gives the average golfer a bad moment. Gary says don't panic. Just stand open, play the ball further back in your stance and close the clubface at address with a sand wedge. Aim three inches behind the ball, take a slow swing with a full shoulder turn and hit down into the sand. The ball will come out pretty well but will roll a lot on landing, so make allowances for this.

The other plugged ball is found in the face of a bunker. The same principles apply but make sure you are well balanced, with the weight 70 per cent on the front foot. The ball will not go all that far from this kind of position, but remember the main purpose — to get out.

I am often asked about the downhill lie in a sandtrap. As a rule the depth of the sand decreases from the point where your club enters, so it is not a bad idea to hit the sand with your club a good four inches behind the ball. Open the clubface and stay down on it by keeping your knees flexed a little.

Gary always used to say that it was inevitable that during a round you would be in a bunker, so if you were confident of getting out, you would adopt a more aggressive attitude with your stroke. They highlighted the green in the same way that fairway bunkers often indicated the best route to the hole. 'The trick is to use your eyes and see what the golf course architect is trying to make you do,' says Gary.

It used to be said that Ben Hogan deliberately played for sand (I wonder) and Gary Player actually wrote that in situations where there was a water hazard on one side of the green and a bunker on the other, he would aim for the sand rather than the water, which meant a one-stroke penalty, no matter what. So he aimed at sand, without fear of the water, and as often as not ended on the green anyway.

Gary says that getting it up and down in two shots (one bunker, one putt) is what the sandtrap business is all about. 'When you think that championships rest on maybe a single stroke, you realise how important it is to get the ball out of trouble, and up alongside the flagstick,' he says. 'The same applies to your local competitions. Practise all types of bunker shots until you have total confidence in your ability to get the ball close, and if anybody calls you lucky with your bunker shots, tell 'em what I tell 'em: 'That's right — the more I practise, the luckier I get!'.' 'But', I hear you say, 'my club hasn't a practice bunker.' Alas, all too true at most of our clubs.

It was said that Vardon, in his prime, played for several years without ever leaving the fairway. However, as an element of luck exists in golf, no matter what anyone says, it is best to be prepared to extract yourself from all troubles. Reg Whitcombe invited everyone to simply try to make sure they got the ball out of the rough and into a playable position; now the stars seem always to be hitting for the flagstick from quite ghastly places.

The most frightening bunkers of course are the really deep ones. Often you cannot see the green or pin and frequently the poor golfer thrashes away at the ball without a positive thought in his head. To escape, you need to hit the ball high in the air and to do this you need an open clubface at

(*right*) Ben Hogan bunkered at Wentworth, 1956 (*Bert Neale*); (*below*) Prestwick, first home of the Open (*Peter Dazeley Photography*)

impact. Pick the club up steeply, keep your eyes focused on the sand a couple of inches behind the ball, and splash it out.

It is no use trying for distance from a deep bunker. It is impossible to hit a high shot a long way — the object is to get out. If it is a greenside bunker, you might get lucky and flip it upwards sharply up to the pin. Give it a good followthrough, believe in yourself and be decisive. Play out backwards if the position is hopeless.

Bunkers in the fairway often require the golfer to hit the ball a hundred yards or more. It is a fact that few practise this shot — in fact very few British courses provide a practice bunker. When there is one, it is something of an apology, usually filled with weed, tucked away among the greenkeeper's tools and a discouraging distance from the clubhouse.

The secret with these longer shots is to play them as you would any other stroke, except that you try to make sure you hit the ball 'clean'. You can try a lofted wood, but I would not recommend it especially if the sand is soft. And you can deliberately hit the ball thin to gain distance, again difficult. But get it out and perhaps leave these shots for the experts.

Sometimes, you see players taking a putter in a bunker. The gallery usually think this means the competitor has lost his nerve but in fact he is playing canny. If the bunker has no lip and the ball can roll out of trouble, this is sensible play; you don't always have to blast it out. Of course the sand must be firm, like it is after rain, and the ball must not be expected to climb up a steep bank, but if the bunker is shallow this is one way out. Try to hit the ball with the putter just below the centre. This will give you the forward spin you will need.

Old-time golfers used this method of recovery sometimes at seaside links, but gradually designers of golf courses built up the bunkers and made them much more fearsome. But even today there are quite shallow 'natural' bunkers and the putter can be the answer. Don't hurry the shot, just give the ball a nice smooth stroke and exaggerate your follow-through to ensure you don't stop the head of the putter after impact.

Incidentally, you can run up a shot from a bunker. Take a 7-iron and place most of your weight on the forward foot. The trick with this stroke is to hit the ball before you hit the sand. Also remember to keep your hands ahead of the clubface. Aim just ahead of the ball, and strike it cleanly, otherwise you will get backspin and the shot will pull up short of the target. You will probably use a little wrist action on this one and it is surprising how successful this bread-and-butter chip shot from a bunker can be. In the old days they got it down to a fine art and were highly skilled in putting the blade into the ball with great precision. All this, of course, before the Sarazen sandblaster took over.

Alliss bunkered

There is nothing more frustrating for the poor golfer than to be continually told that bunker shots are the easiest shots in golf. To the first-class professional and good club golfer the shot is a relatively easy one, but I could think of several top pros who are none too brilliant in greenside bunkers.

The main thing, of course, for the average golfer, is to select a club which is best suited to the sand on the course where he plays. If you play on a heavy clay course you want a sand iron with a rather sharp leading edge. If your golf is played mainly on a seaside course where the sand is soft and powdery, a club with a bigger, heavier flange will not dig too deeply into the sand.

Once you have a suitable club for the sand, you can begin to learn the rudiments of bunker play. Like all shots from twenty or thirty yards, the great secret is to take a long enough backswing. A great number of people flick at balls in the sand trying to 'pick' them off the top with no backswing, or they have a vast long backswing and thump right into the sand behind the ball hoping for some miracle to occur.

You will see that most top players have a considerable backswing and follow through. They do not jab into the sand behind the ball.

(*left*) Ken Bousfield flicks one clean near the 16th green at Wentworth, 1950 (*Sport & General*); (*right*) Dai Rees would have been happy just to get it back on the fairway from this position

I have always favoured the slightly open stance with the ball well forward on the left foot; let the arms swing along the line of the toes with the blade slightly open, that is aiming slightly to the left of the target with the shoulders and feet but by opening the club face slightly so that it is towards the flag. Then come a little outside on the backswing and across in the follow-through, keeping the body still. Let the arms go through to a nice high finish and the ball should come out quite easily.

Certain bunker shots, of course, are not easy, such as if the ball is on a down slope at the back of the bunker and the pin near to you, or the ball under the lip with nowhere for you to stand. These are difficult for the expert, let alone the handicap player.

There are ways and means, however, of overcoming these problems but they do take practice and that is what the great majority of club golfers will not do, even if there are practice facilities. I do not think I saw more than two members in my thirteen years at Parkstone practising bunker shots and yet they probably have to play two or three every time they go out to play.

I have never believed in chipping out of a bunker, even when the sand is hard. Putting out yes, provided you have a dead straight bunker with no lip and the sand hard-packed. If you can knock it out with a putter all well and good but for most of the time I always imagine a slight bank in front of me, even though it is a flat bunker and just play a normal shot over this imaginary bank, but there again this calls for practice and experimenting.

From the rough

Heather
Just before we reach the putting green, a friend has asked how to recover from really heavy rough. He thinks professionals have some magical way of getting out of jungle and is particularly interested in how to extract himself from the heather.

Heather and rough can cause the average golfer a great deal of trouble, but let us get this clear — nobody should ever be frightened of the stuff. Even the best of players get into it, and out again.

The ability to play recovery shots is vital to anyone who wishes to become a better than average golfer; most players, when faced with a longish shot out of rough are too greedy and try to play the wrong shot with the wrong club.

Let's first take shots from heather round the green. The key to this shot is 'swing the club'. Never under any circumstances try and hit the ball out with a short quick jab.

I always liken this in many ways to the bunker shot; the hands should be

66

at least between the hip and shoulder at the top of the backswing. Now, even if you just drop the club on the ball, it will be sufficient to send the ball quite a distance, so remember: don't flick or snatch at the ball.

Also bear in mind that when you are playing out of heather you are most certain to get a cushion of it between the club face and the ball; this will have the effect of taking nearly all the backspin off the shot so never get the idea that you will be able to pitch right up to the flag and stop.

Then again you must not try to baby it out of the heather. The odds are that you will miss-hit the shot and end up having to try again.

But never be afraid of heather; your iron is much tougher than it is and if you play the shot right you should escape without tears or trouble. Get the distance in your mind's eye and try to picture yourself rolling the ball up to the hole.

For longer shots out of heather you need a different technique. Of course, if the lie is very bad, always take the simplest and shortest route to safety. 'Cut your losses' must be the order of the day and use even a sand iron, keeping the hands well forward during the swing.

Study the shot carefully and never take stupid risks. If you feel the shot will come off with a stronger club then by all means play it, but if any doubts creep in adopt safety first tactics every time. Keep a cool head at all times.

Grass
A majority of courses contain no heather but all (except for a few in the Middle East) have plenty of grass. In playing out of rough, the first thing to do is think, and think realistically. This does not mean I am telling you to be over-cautious but that you must weigh up what you intend the result to be and how you can best achieve that aim.

Let us assume you have missed the fairway on a par 5 and want to get as much length on your second shot as possible. First you must examine the lie carefully. If you are lucky, it may be 'sitting up' in an even better position than if you were on the closer-cut turf of the fairway. If this is so, you might even attempt a driver shot but for the majority of golfers it would be unwise to use anything more than a 3-wood, as much because the driver's length of shaft is more difficult to control than anything else.

Once the ball begins to settle down in the grass, however, the problems become very different, the difference between, in fact, taking a wood or a very lofted iron indeed. My advice to you is from a good lie use the club you have the most confidence in. For many golfers this is likely to be a 4- or even 5-wood, but remember to sweep it away: if you hit down at the ball a skied shot could well be the result and a carry of only fifty or so yards. If the lie is poor, your goals must become far more limited and a long iron becomes the club you really should not attempt; unless you have very fast hand action and equally great power and control. So a rule of thumb is to use a wood from reasonable lies in the rough and almost immediately drop down to no more than a 6-iron once the lie is not entirely clean.

Once the ball becomes 'well settled', you should be thinking only of moving it to somewhere more favourable — just back to the fairway. At this point, think of using the most lofted clubs in your bag. A sand wedge is often the best answer.

If your ball is really buried in thick grass, here is a tip that I find works for me. Don't attempt to swing directly at the ball; approach your shot exactly as if you were in a bunker and aim about two inches behind the ball. This time, instead of sand exploding the ball out of trouble, your divot does it for you. Of course you won't get much length on the shot but it will get you those few vital yards back to the fairway.

For shots close up to the green, where you aim is to get your ball close to the flag, what I have already said as regards playing out of heather will still apply. But always be willing to cut your losses and use your handicap — that's what it's for!

Putting is like love

Millions of words have been written about putting. There have been books devoted to the subject while I, personally, have suffered the agonies of the damned on the greens although I can't have been as bad as some 'friends' made out as I won twenty major tournaments. Some say putting is a game within a game, unconnected with golf and quite intelligent players have said the putting part of golf isn't fair, or the hole should be bigger. Others have been reduced to jelly by the dreaded yips.

So let's talk about those methods which worked and examine the magicians of the green. I'm not going to mince words; the best putter I ever saw was Bobby Locke from South Africa. There are other super putters, and we'll look at them later, but Locke, to me, was the master and had the ability to get the ball rolling 'over itself' and on line in an uncanny way.

Did Locke top his putts, hook them or was it his wonderful touch? I suspect a little of everything.

Bobby Locke stood over the ball with a closed stance, seemed to hold the shaft lightly in his fingers and took the blade back square to the hole throughout the swing. Many said he 'hooded' the blade on the swing back. What seems certain was that the blade was always facing the target and that he did not need to roll the wrists or compensate in any way. In this manner

68

Late in his career Vardon became agonised over any short putt — perhaps a result of too many years putting on greens like these . . .

he made putting look easy and, being brought up on South African greens which in those days had a lot of nap on them, he'd become observant in regard to the direction the grass was growing, knew what 'shine' meant on a green, or the 'matt look'. Grass cut 'away' from you means the ball rolls more freely on the slippery surface and the 'matt' look means the grass has been cut towards you, and your ball rolls against the grain. Some golfers never bother to think about these points or to look at the overall slope and shape of a green, which have great bearing on how a ball will roll.

Reg Whitcombe used to say we should all be at great pains to study the line over which the ball is to travel. Do a little gardening: remove fine stones thrown up by greenside bunker shots, leaves, twigs and so on.

If you're going to fail to sink a putt, fail to sink it *past the hole*. In other words if your ball doesn't reach the hole, it's never going to drop. As that great putter of long ago, Willie Park, said 'As long as you live the hole will never come to the ball.' Charlie Ward practised his putting endlessly with 20 balls and, if he left one short, he made himself start again. He scolded himself and, consequently, was seldom short!

Modern pros practise their putting for hours on end. I've seen Gary Player tapping them in during darkness and Lee Trevino has worn out more hotel carpets than his manager dare admit. Go back over the years and you find James Braid growling that the majority of golfers didn't take their putting seriously enough. If they did, he'd say, they would be very much the better for it.

Braid said more than seventy years ago what a modern master, Billy Casper, said only the other week. If you want to cut shots off your round, the quickest way is to practise your putting! But I don't think Casper would have approved the Braid method of putting with an open stance, and the blade opening on the backswing. But the great old man obviously had a wonderful rhythm and touch that must have seen him happily across those difficult Walton Heath greens.

In the old days the pros trotted out some curious ideas. Jack White, at Sunningdale, used to tell his assistants to putt the ball from the toe for a right-to-left putt, and from the heel for the reverse slope. Can you imagine the confusion! Today I am here to tell you that every putt is dead straight. Not necessarily for the hole, but straight on your selected line. There's no mystique to this and anyone who putts from other than the 'sweet spot' on the blade is asking for trouble. Of course, there are always exceptions with genius. What about that Japanese player, Aoki, who sticks the toe of the putter in the air and gives it a wristy jerk into the middle every time? Let him get on with it, say I. But go for the simple style every time. Don't bend over in knots or stand miles wide unless it really does work for you.

When you go to a tournament study the way the good putters move about on the green. You'll notice they mostly approach the ball from behind. One or two will look at the line from the hole back towards the ball. Sam Snead said he looked at the ball with his master eye, which happened to be his left, toes parallel with the line, hands held in close and the ball placed plumb centre of the blade, with all of the base of the club flat on the turf.

On a fast downhill putt Snead maintained he held the putter more lightly than on an uphill putt. He said his wrists did the work and at no time is there any body action in putting (unlike Locke, who swayed). He swung the blade easily and firmly accelerated into the ball. All very simple and when you read this you must wonder how on earth some of us made such a hash of it. As dear Henry Longhurst used to say: 'If you've got the twitch you've got it and there's no cure!'

The man who can putt is a match for anyone. So said Willie Park, winner of the Open in 1887 and 1889. And, from all accounts, Mr Park had utmost confidence in his ability and at one time said there was not a better putter than himself in the world. He regarded putting as an art, but said it could be

(*opposite*) Isao Aoki with toe in the air. Note that he does not use the more usual reverse overlap grip (*Peter Dazeley Photography*)

acquired. He played matches for money, and on some occasions this was £100, a fortune in those days. Park said he belonged to a race of Scottish professionals whose matches for big money stakes made some of the most illuminating pages in the history of the game. You might have said he was self-assured, even conceited, about his ability with a putter. And this, I feel certain, was the reason he putted so well. He believed in himself and beat J. H. Taylor, as well as giving Vardon a terrible time with some deadly putting. Park kept saying, almost until he bored everyone, that he had proved that a man who can putt is a match for anyone, and a man who can't putt is a match for nobody!

Park liked a putter with a little loft, and a long shaft which had to be stiff. The grip should be thin as this gives a better feel. On slow greens, he liked a heavy putter, but did not recommend changing putters as you move about the country. He gripped in two-handed fashion, but his hands were close together. He said the left hand merely guided the putter and the right hand strikes the ball. The fingers played a vital part in the Park method and he was obviously a man with a very superior touch. And he knew it!

Where Park moved away from our ideas of 'sensible' putting was in his stance. He played the ball off the right foot, standing wide open. Bear in mind he had a lofted putter and that greens weren't nearly as well kept as they are today.

Although our Mr Park had a long-shafted putter, he ran his hands well down the shaft and bent his body well over the ball with the eyes directly above the blade. He told golfers that those unaccustomed to stooping will feel a sensation of blood rushing to the head and to eradicate this weakness they should practise putting in a crouched position — odd chap! However, we must remain respectful. This man was the greatest putter of his day and had some advice which holds good a hundred years on. Only raise the putter blade high enough on the backswing to keep it clear of the ground. The putter, he said, should only hit the ball and not the ball and the ground together. At one time Park used to raise the blade and rest the heel on the turf. He found this effective in helping to keep the ball rolling close to the turf. Why did he give it up? After putting four hours a day with six balls in practice, he progressed to a more orthodox method which was striking the putt almost a descending blow — with that lofted club, remember.

He said he took the putter blade back slowly and struck the ball in a 'kindly' way from the dead centre of the blade. He did not look up to see if the ball was going in, but expected it to do so and looked up when he thought it would be reaching the hole.

Park considered the short putt as any length up to five feet. For this he said the wrists do all the work and the body and arms should be kept still.

Also, in drawing the club back, the eye can be kept on the direction in which it is going, without looking away from the ball. The follow-through should be decisive and should be stopped after six inches. But there should be no jerk. No wavering. And no irresolute finish to the stroke. The movement throughout is slow and steady, and its termination must be definite.

So now you know. Where Park is confusing is that he claimed there were three ways into a hole: straight, hooked, or sliced. Have nothing to do with this, say I!

If you get desperate about putting, and don't we all at some time, you might like to know that Joe Turnesa once won the Metropolitan Open in America, putting one-handed. This made such an impact round the New York area that club members tried to copy him. However, Joe later began to miss a few, so went back to two-handed putting.

Another sure-fire tip in America was put into practice by Bobby Cruickshank, who shot scores of 67 and 68 putting while looking at the hole, not the ball. In fact he became most excited about this new discovery, until the third round, where he five-putted one green — end of experiment!

I've tried the reverse grip with the left hand below the right and it worked well. I reached a stage in my golf career when I would have willingly tried anything on the greens, except perhaps the trick American Harry Cooper pulled before the war. He produced a pair of spectacles which made the hole appear bigger. It didn't last. Once Walter Hagen was beaten in a putting contest by an elderly lady in Australia and in 1946 the great Ben Hogan missed a putt of about three feet which would have tied him for the US Open.

Weekenders often fail to understand why top pros miss seemingly innocent-looking short putts. I like the story of the club member who boasted he could knock in a six-footer similar to the one missed by a great champion. 'Come on' he said, 'I'll do it now.' A big bet was struck, but the putt was delayed. It was decided it would be hit next week to give the boastful chap time to think about it. When the day arrived a great fuss was made measuring six feet with a tape measure. A crowd was allowed to gather and would the putting ace mind if photos were taken? Someone let loose a dog and generally all the commotion of a tournament was reproduced. You guessed. He missed.

It's in America that there have been some quite incredible feats of putting. Billy Casper can tell of the day Bob Rosburg needed only 19 putts on eighteen holes while shooting a 62 in the Pensacola Open and that might well be the all-time record!

If you had watched Rosburg drive a ball you might have been

unimpressed. He used the two-handed grip and just gave the ball a thump, sometimes hitting it a touch thin. But once on the green he had an astonishing touch, plus a fine positive attitude.

So good a putter was he that they insisted he wrote a book all about it, and if you read it you'll find that he once scored a round of 59 in an exhibition match and had eight one-putt greens in the first nine, and twenty-three in all. When he won the 1959 PGA Championship, match-play then, they said he putted the daylights out of his opponents.

Some think putting plays too important a role in the game. Gary Player admits to thinking this on occasions but refuses to join a campaign to devalue the putt, or have a larger hole! Gary spent hundreds of hours practising his putts and used to say: 'This for the British Open. This for the British Open.'

While Casper putted with something of a wristy tap, others swing the blade. Rosburg, the magician, kept all his fingers of the right hand on the grip and photos of him show he sometimes plunged his left thumbnail into the grip. Always the back of the left hand faced the target and always the blade was kept low with a flowing stroke accelerating into the ball, which then rolled away with purpose. His head was kept perfectly still and he said if you looked up too soon you would ruin the stroke. But once these experts lost their genius on the greens, they faded away. And don't I know the feeling!

There have been wonderful putters in America over the years, and many have been taught. But how many times have you seen a professional giving a putting lesson? Yet this is half the game and a good method is all important.

Turn once again to *Methods of Teaching*, that American PGA instructional book, and you'll be interested to read that teachers there have more tolerance of methods of putting that differ from the top pros. In my opinion this is a mistake because a weekender, never exposed to much pressure, can get away with a cranky method. But ask him to hole a five-footer for £10 on the last green, and then watch him jerk it past the hole. What I'm saying is that it is a wise golfer who learns a functional and simple way to putt because such a method will hold him in good stead when the heat is on. This means that if a weekender needs a 4 at the last hole to win the monthly medal, at least he won't make an ass of himself on the green.

The American advice is to play the ball from wherever the distribution of weight lies. In other words if you stand with most of your weight on the left foot, position the ball there. Most good putters, says the US book, keep the blade low to the ground during the entire swing to make the blade accelerate into the ball. The stroke is smooth with no head or body movement. The wrists may be rigid throughout, or may be slightly flexible. The reverse overlap grip seems most popular in the USA but no teacher is dogmatic about this and it pays to experiment and make your own choice.

My advice is to stand fairly upright to the ball and try to get putts to roll smoothly with no hopping — easier written than done!

My father Percy was an excellent putter when young and in his book *Better Golf* maintained that the putt was the easiest stroke to learn which, as things turned out, I found hard to swallow as putting was not exactly my strongest point! He claimed that in putting you should allow for the occasional personal peculiarity but said you should always remember there are certain main points which underlie good putting. He said the feet should not be more than six inches apart and insisted that the player should have a clear view to the hole, not so simple if an over-wide stance is adopted. Like other sensible players, he would have nothing to do with any writer who recommended that you spin the ball on the green. He liked a direct strike from the centre of the blade and he was unusual in adopting the same grip of the putter as he did with the other clubs.

The length of my father's backswing depended on the length of the putt but he told his pupils and readers that they should tend towards a shorter backswing with the putter, rather than a longer one which has worked for some, like Ken Bousfield in my playing days, but not for others I could mention. The part of the ball that should be looked at is the back. Head and elbows remain motionless throughout the action and the hole should never be watched out of the corner of the eye.

I rather like my father's advice about putting on an undulating green. He would step well away from the ball and fix his eye on a spot over which he felt the ball should roll, and the putt would be made with this in mind. It always pays, he said, to exaggerate the angle at which the putt is made, or the line wide of the hole, simply because when the amount of fall or break is underestimated, the ball will always run well past. Better, then, to aim on the high side and at least finish stone dead.

Father Alliss was dogmatic in his book. He believed the best putting was achieved with an aluminium-headed putter. He also had one piece of advice to me — and you. Practise a great deal!

Broadly speaking I have found the best and most consistent putters have been the ones with the simplest method. The 1923 British Amateur Champion, Roger Wethered, used to say he never looked at a rival competitor except on the green and that was to see how the other chap's ball rolled, and this to learn about pace, or see how the ball took the break.

Years ago Willie Park and the American winner of the 1904 British Amateur, Walter Travis, always practised their putting into a smaller than

One of the best British amateurs in the 1920s and 1930s: Roger Wethered with the Amateur Championship cup

usual hole. When they putted on the course into a normal sized hole, it looked as big as a bucket. So that's a thought for your practice putting green.

The mental approach is important. Jack Nicklaus said that as in alligator wrestling, the approach is everything! You must believe in yourself and think in a positive way. You know you can hole any putt of any length because you've seen others do it. Maybe you can't drive 300 yards but you can hole a thirty-footer because you've seen it done by weekend golfers.

Right. Having established that fact, the next thing we learn from the masters is that they take their time. Nicklaus would stare at the hole, transfixed. Bobby Locke studied the grain at the hole and always had the same routine. Ken Brown wanders around the green; Trevino paces restlessly. Some wipe the blade, tug at their trousers, give a half-smile, place the blade in front of the ball. All good putters have a routine of sorts.

Now let's get personal. You may choose to putt with your wrists or your shoulders. You may reckon it's all done with the arms. But do what is natural to you in this connection but please, whatever else you do, make sure the putter is accelerating into the ball.

How you hold the club is up to you. Most say you should have both thumbs down the top of the shaft and the top American putters favoured the reverse overlap grip while some excellent putters, Dai Rees is an example, favoured the two-handed grip with all the fingers on the leather.

My advice about putters is to get hold of a good traditional design and stick with it. On the other hand you constantly hear of top-liners hitting a winning streak, thanks to changing putters. Some years ago Max Faulkner used to make his own putters, once out of some driftwood, and he did rather well, winning the 1951 Open title at Royal Portrush. But basically, play safe with a sensible non-gimmicky putter and hope it has just a little loft on the blade.

Sam Snead used to say that once any golfer was on the green he could be a match for anyone. There was no reason why a club duffer could not beat the daylights out of the champion. Touch and plenty of practice is all you need. Like Locke, Snead took the blade back totally square, or 'hooded' if you prefer. The ball would seldom hop away when he putted. He claimed concentration, confidence and relaxation were the keys to good putting and demonstrated this all over the world. He said we should eliminate all outside thoughts as we lined up a putt and had only to decide the line to the hole. He didn't want us to second-guess it as the Americans say — once we have decided the line we should stick with that decision no matter what.

Snead advised that we might try to experiment with stance. In later years he did this himself, when the twitch got him, first putting from between the legs and when that was banned using the side-saddle line-up. Arnold Palmer in the early 1960s used to putt brilliantly from a knock-kneed stance where both knees almost touched each other, not to stop them from shaking, but to eliminate any risk of sway — very sensible in a high wind!

Snead looked a smooth putter at his peak. His feet were about twelve inches apart, knees slightly bent and the back of his left hand faced the hole. He didn't flap at the ball, or jerk it there. Everything about his putting was smooth with the ball being struck with the centre of the blade.

As the cash rewards grew for golf, so the efficiency of the competitors on the green blossomed and we began to see quite astonishing feats of putting. The 1951 Open, for instance, was won with probably fewer putts than any Open before, Max Faulkner needing just twenty-four putts in one round, and an average of twenty-nine in the three others! He claimed a lightweight putter and holding the grip in the fingers were the secret, and he also said too many club members picked the putter up somewhat sharply on the back swing.

Bobby Locke obviously made professionals realise that it wasn't cheating to roll in the ball from all angles. After downing quite the most extraordinary putts Locke would touch his white cap, and walk majestically to the next tee with barely a flicker.

In the early 1960s a New Zealand left-hander came along and, although he had a curtailed back swing, putted like a wizard, making it all look very simple. He was so frightening that in one World Match-Play championship Hale Irwin admitted he looked away and almost cringed when Bob Charles was putting.

The respect in which Charles was held on the greens lasted at least ten years. There was no question that Charles could give three shots a round to the best of his rivals. He simply got the ball into the hole in fewer shots than others thought reasonable.

Charles always reckoned that putting was a straight-forward business and that all you do is return the blade square to the ball, having kept it pretty square to the target throughout the swing. Once the simple method is established you practise a lot until feel and touch develops, along with utter confidence that if the ball doesn't drop it is probably no fault of the striker.

Charles said good putting is ten per cent method and ninety per cent mental and that you must believe, every time you stand over the ball, that you are going to hole it. He thinks you must assess a putt even before walking on to the green. You look at the surrounding land as very often this will give a clue as to how a ball will roll. Greens often 'lean' towards a river, road or depression, even though they may look reasonably flat. He advises against spending overlong looking at the line as this can create indecision. Once you've made up your mind how the ball will break, go right ahead and play the shot. Nine times out of ten your first reading of a line will be the correct one.

The business of feel, so often lost on really good golfers, is created by transmitting what your eye tells you to your hands. On long putts Charles might pace out the distance from ball to hole, as this helped tell him how hard to hit the putt. Charles admits this might not work for everyone and points out that Lee Trevino prefers to prowl around a long putt, looking for all the angles before settling himself.

Simplicity of stroke allied to the confidence which comes from continual practice were the watch-words of Bob Charles at his best and his whole approach to putting set an example to others who wanted to cut their scores dramatically.

It was in the World Match-Play of 1979 at Wentworth that we saw so many remarkable displays of putting under pressure. In the autumn the greens there tend to be soft, but true, and old campaigners like Gary Player came to know them better than most. We saw Bill Rogers of America, almost unknown in Britain, win thanks almost entirely to a super, delightfully simple putting method. This slim-line chap, who weighs only 10 stones, does not hit the ball as far as some fellow-professionals, but once he is on the green he displays an eye for reading the line, and a touch to go with it.

(left) Bill Rogers: reverse overlap grip *(Peter Dazeley Photography)*; *(right)* Hands apart from Hubert Green *(Peter Dazeley Photography)*

Don't think for a minute that I'm insisting that all golfers should stick with the classical, simple putting method. It seems that sound methods, however, just might put less strain on a competitor, although this would be hard to prove. Nobody could ever say Locke putted in a modern manner. He used a wooden-shafted putter and wooden clubs, as Henry Cotton says, caused all kinds of problems in the old days. (Crossing the Atlantic Cotton had to put his wooden-shafted clubs in a bucket of water because the ship's drying air, he said, meant the heads might work loose.) Bobby Locke never mentioned a loose putting head, but his rivals almost lost theirs, against him! In America some said he stabbed the turf, almost took a divot — which wasn't true — others said that he hooked that ball into the hole. But he did take the money with that weak left hand!

Other unusual putters include Isao Aoki from Japan and Hubert Green, the likeable American. Both, Aoki in particular, stick the heel of the putter into the turf so that the toe points skywards. Green separates his hands and almost always this method worked. I say 'almost' because I cannot erase from my mind his missed putt on the 72nd hole in the 1978 US Masters. It was three feet and if he had holed it, he would have tied. Aoki, however, seems to hole many vital strokes with his eccentric method so we come back to the point Charles makes — putting is mostly mental.

The most famous putting lapse of the last decade or so was by Doug Sanders who had 'this for the Open' in 1970. 'This' was a three foot six incher, but the drama had started before the green was reached. The trouble was a pitch shot which went to the back of the green. Three putts from there is likely for anyone. Poor Sanders missed that second putt. All he had needed was a 4 to win and I can think of few golfers who would not admit that a 4 at the 18th at St Andrews is pretty straightforward.

To conclude our thoughts on putting, I think it wrong to compare old-time putters with the moderns. From pictures of past 'greats', the way they stood and so on, I find it hard to believe they had putting down to the art form it is today. Additionally the greens were less good, as we can tell from the occasional reference to weed.

The best approach putter I've seen must be Nicklaus although, in his day, Palmer got a few in from almost off the green. Big strong types often putt well. Some of us will not forget the way Harry Weetman stroked the ball into the hole with the minimum of fuss. Walter Hagen and Gene Sarazen could putt well, but I wonder whether they would have lived against Locke, Bob Charles, Bill Rogers, Tom Watson, Severiano Ballesteros and the next superstar to come along.

We shall never know. I rather like what Frank Beard once said: You only play as well as your competition and if you played in the company of people who scored 72, then you became good enough to beat them, and scored 71. 'You shoot 71 because that's what it takes to win. For a man to succeed and reach his best, he has to be goaded and you're only as good as your goaders!'

So the conclusion is that you have to play where the best are. And Frank Beard used to say the best golfers play in America so if you want to reach the top, you have to go to the USA. But just how, I wonder, do we translate that thought into Spanish and Japanese?

Tommy Armour, the great Scotsman who won the United States and British Open titles, as well as the US PGA said he had been an eager experimenter with putting all his life and searched for what he called 'The Great Answer' until his final days on this earth. He reckoned you can use any grip you like, take any stance you fancy but insisted that to become a good putter you had to keep the head dead still and make the putter blade go accurately towards the hole. You can spend your days searching for the magic wand but in the end it probably is a wiser investment to spend the time practising the actual putting. Armour won the US Open with a putter he bought one week before the off. Fourteen days later the club began to disappoint him, so he gave it away! Said Armour, 'Love and putting are mysteries for the philosophers to solve. Both subjects are beyond golfers.'

I suppose nobody has had more than his share of problems with this particular department than I have. I now use a reverse grip, that is the right hand at the top of the shaft overlapping with the last two fingers of the left hand. Rather like the normal grip employed by Harry Bradshaw, but in reverse.

There are all sorts of stances, grips, and a hundred and one different shapes of putter. Flat ones, upright ones, light ones, heavy ones. They have all been tried.

Here again it is a question of getting a putter that suits you. You very rarely, or never in fact, see a good workman with bad tools. They may look rusty and old and hickory-shafted, but as soon as you pick them up they have some magical quality about them. I remember Bobby Locke's putter: as soon as you picked it up the balance and feel were something to marvel at — a beautiful club like a Stradivarius violin.

I have tried all the putting stances over the years but I seem to do my best with a relatively narrow one. I think it is important to think in a forward direction. Again roll the ball towards the hole. Do not jab it or try to consciously hit it hard. Here again I think it is a question of feel and practice.

All shots have to be struck with authority and rhythm and the putt, by the mere fact that it is a much gentler shot, has to be timed (even a three-footer), and it is very important that the clubhead should be travelling quicker at impact than it has done at any time in the backswing. Once you start to decelerate, then the shoulders move, the head moves and the ball just will not go in the hole.

Weight is largely a matter of individual preference but if normally you putt on very slow greens you need a fairly heavy putter, but if your greens are fast and slick a medium to light-weight putter may give the best results.

A lot of the very good putters hit the ball half-way up to make sure the top half of the ball moves towards the hole first. I am sure this was one of Locke's great secrets — hitting the top half of the ball and getting it to roll forward, hugging the ground.

Without doubt the short game is the most fascinating part of golf. Oh yes it is nice to hit a ball 300 yards or 200 yards or whatever your horizons are, but it is just as important to play a crisp chip shot, a precision bunker shot and hole a putt from seven or eight feet.

All this you can do if you are prepared to give it a little bit of your time. You will enjoy your golf a lot more and what is more your four-ball partners will as well.

Blueprint for a superman

Most of us are convinced we could hit the ball at least twenty-five yards further if our local pro would unlock our real talent with the secret. When the carbon-fibre shaft arrived in Britain with the promise of further distance off the tee, hundreds leaped for it, despite an £80 price tag.

It is said carbon improves performance because the shaft is considerably lighter and allows more weight to be alloted to the head of the club. The lowering of the centre of gravity that results also has a bearing on clubhead speed. We were told by scientists that in the case of the average golfer using a driver with a steel shaft, clubhead speed is 140 feet per second and should achieve a shot of 200 yards.

The same man increases clubhead speed to 150 feet per second, which means a 217 yard drive, by switching to carbon.

So why, you ask, don't all the professional experts use carbon? I ask the same question. We know Tommy Horton has won with it, and Hedley Muscroft found an extra 75 yards, but is there some snag, just as there was with aluminium which died the death a few years ago? In this case there was a very practical reason. Although the shafts were lighter and gave improved performance as regards length, they also broke with alarming frequency. Look around the workshop at your local pro's shop and you'll find the odd old club, dating back to the 1940s and 1950s. Its steel shaft may no longer be a pretty sight because of rust but the club will still be usable. Not so with aluminium. The woods lasted quite well — a friend of mine is playing still with a set but not so for the irons. After a year or so of use, they began to break where there is most stress — just above the hosel. Carbon-fibre has proved to be tougher, though breakages still occur. In this case though, I think the problem is the difference of feel, which means that the golfer feels he has to use a slightly different swing for his driver with its carbon shaft than the rest of his set — and we've been saying how the basic swing should remain the same for each club. Some with the cash to spare have done the obvious thing and bought the whole set — I recall Johnny Miller so equipped a few years ago when he won the 1976 Open at Birkdale — but few have persisted with them, including Miller himself.

So it seems that equipment alone has few answers and it's certainly difficult to believe that clubs have improved all that much since the steel shaft reached a high level of performance years ago. Think too of all the gimmicky iron clubheads we've been seeing for several years now. Yet what is the present trend? A return to the traditional blade without all those humps and hollows on the back.

I think for golf equipment there have been just two revolutionary

(*left*) Peter Thomson in the final round of the 1961 Dunlop Masters at Royal Porthcawl (*Bert Neale*); (*right*) Severiano Ballesteros at St Andrews in the 1978 Open. The next year he won it and followed up with the US Masters (*Michael Hobbs*)

innovations. The first was Mr Haskell's wound ball early this century, which rapidly banished the gutty from the scene; the other was the steel shaft around 1930. Both had similar effects on the game. They made it easier for the duffer and enabled the better-class player to hit the ball much further — say a hundred yards on the drive.

So for a few decades we've seen nothing truly revolutionary and if someone does come along with a new piece of magic I'm pretty certain that the ruling bodies of British and American golf will step in and ban it . . . . In any event, do we really want to see every putt holed or golf courses stretched to 10,000 yards because someone has produced a club that will propel a ball 400 yards?

Perhaps in the future we may see a revolution in the golfer. If only we could build a bionic golfer, a Mr Unbeatable, what would the result look like? Maybe a combination of Nicklaus, Snead and Hogan for the long shots with a dash of Bobby Locke and Billy Casper for the pitches and chips, plus a touch of Tom Watson or Bob Charles for the putting?

There are other requirements for superman golfer. He'd have to be unbeatable in every part of the world, give his best on every occasion, on every type of course, in all kinds of weather and while eating foods of bewildering variety. And he should be unflappable in every situation. Maybe Gary Player came nearest to this.

Ability alone might not be enough. It's no good, for instance, for Mr Super Golfer to get round in the low 60s all the time and then blow it with the public, or the press afterwards. He would need to be diplomatic and would undoubtedly need a manager to get him extra work, contracts with the best people; someone to boost him and to ensure money poured into both their pockets by every possible means. All this might mean he would soon be burnt out as a human being and golfer, but it would be worthwhile making hay while the sun shone and essential, too, because the tax man grabs away continuously throughout the Western World.

Henry Cotton, who won three Open titles and has earned money from the game for years and years — and still does at the age of seventy-three — was asked what kind of blueprint was required for a super champion. His reply was: 'The star should be handsome, around six feet, weigh thirteen stone or a little less, and be naturally strong with a wiry sort of toughness.'

Besides actual strength Superman Golfer must have speed of hand, says Cotton, and must be able to make it look easy, just as Roberto de Vicenzo did. This Argentinian golfer came nearest, said Henry, to what he thought the ideal should be.

Cotton said long fingers were essential and he even insisted they should be impeccably manicured. He wanted the star to be highly intelligent and have had a good level of education and perfect manners. He might also have to overcome the problems of a vivid imagination and the other difficulties encountered in golf by those with a sensitive disposition.

Our champion should be able to fit into any company and know about things other than golf. He should appreciate life, art, wine, travel, languages, books, theatre, music and opera — but not too profoundly as he would be very busy. Varied interests are essential if the champion is to avoid being a crashing bore when not in golfing company. In this respect, of modern stars, Peter Thomson is good value. He never felt that golf was the whole of life and has even been seen to read literature from China and histories of India.

Should a young champion marry, or wait? Cotton maintains that these days, when a golfer has to play in tournaments all over the world all the year, a top-line golfer needs companionship and should certainly be able to carry the responsibilities of a wife. This, additionally, will put fewer temptations in the way of a healthy and virile athlete.

Turnberry — a large crowd watching play on the 5th green during the Open Golf
Championship in 1977, won by Tom Watson (*Bert Neale*)

(*above*) St Andrews — the Old Course with a view of the 18th green and the clubhouse (*Bert Neale*); (*below*) Walton Heath — the 2nd hole (*Bert Neale*)

Our man would have to be dedicated and keep up his general muscle tone with exercises, and he would have to take care not to become deformed physically because of endless practice. One reason few golfers stay good for long is that they have to contort and almost practise themselves out of an ideal body. Henry himself developed a marked left-to-right slope as a result of unremitting hours of practice in the right-shoulder-down golf stance. Contra exercises to correct this have been advocated for years.

Cotton thought his super player should come from the amateur ranks and insisted his man win there before turning professional. Lanny Wadkins and Ben Crenshaw are two recent examples, Nicklaus another. He should have been a good enough amateur such as was the great Irishman, Joe Carr, to back himself with his own money, and be confident under pressure. Lee Trevino was such a pressure player. Although not an amateur champion, as a young professional he played anyone who came along for more money than Lee could afford to lose.

Years ago Tommy Armour bet on himself in such a way that he had to shoot in the mid-60s to make money. Snead also used to set up bets which required him to score a 68 or better — or pay up. This 'play well, or pay' policy must be part of the education of a special golfer and has, maybe, been lacking in British golf.

Possibly Arnold Palmer came as near to anyone in the history of the game as the man who best filled the Superman category, although he won the US Open only once, hitting destructive shots on several occasions when he had played himself into the lead. However he was the most marketable golfer since Walter Hagen and even when he reached 50 still drew large crowds. When the Australians asked him to play in their Seniors event, his manager asked for a colossal fee — but did not get it according to the newspapers of the day.

But because of Palmer's magnetism, products bearing his name, some having no connection with golf, sell well and will continue to do so, long after his death and in just the same way as golf products still sell for Walter Hagen. Likewise, the Nicklaus name is very big marketing. He had to work at it though. Once known among his fellow professionals on the US tour as 'The Fat Boy', his rather unfashionable figure meant that he was hardly a suitable male model for the advertising men to display in a new season's shirts, slacks and sweaters. So towards the end of the 1960s he slimmed down, abandoned his crew cut and became highly marketable. Nicklaus is now a colossal money-earner and because of all the titles he has won will continue to outsell future champions long after he has retired.

There have been other contenders for Mr Superman Golfer. Tom Weiskopf of America strides along the fairways like an erect guardsman, but

(*left*) Winner of the 1973 Open at Troon, Tom Weiskopf (and a beard!) trying a rigid fore-finger to stop the left wrist breaking (*Peter Dazeley Photography*); (*right*) Mr Superman, Tom Watson (*Peter Dazeley Photography*)

if things start to go wrong he loses heart and temper and on more than one occasion has batted the ball across the green. In a World Open he even four-putted from three feet or so, from annoyance and frustration. Even so, it is hard to understand why he has won only one of the four classics, in his case the 1973 British Open and, for Tom perhaps it is now too late.

If you were very lucky enough to dine with old champion Henry Cotton he would tell you that destiny plays a part in everyone's lives and that is the only way he was able to explain why Sam Snead failed to win his own US Open. Possibly it was down in the book that he would not win what Snead himself would regard as the most important title in golf.

Yet there is still one candidate of today that I have not named, Tom Watson. Palmer began his pilgrimages to the British Open in 1960 and very soon the event undoubtedly became the major championship with the most international field of them all. As regards the US entry alone, instead of two or three visitors, we now see most of the top players competing. So in the last twenty years who has the best record of them all? For sheer consistency you would have to give it to Nicklaus, who every year finishes high and has won it three times: 1966 at Muirfield and 1970 and 1978 at St Andrews. But this has been over nearly twenty years. Young Tom's first appearance was at Carnoustie in 1975, where he won, and he has followed with victories at Turnberry in a head-to-head with Nicklaus over the last two rounds in 1977 and then at Muirfield in 1980. Looking back now at that last victory perhaps we can agree that it was the sort of victory we might expect from our Mr Superman. On the first day the weather was wet, windy and cold; many golfers saw their hopes fade away. At the end of the day Watson was in the lead with a 68, equalled by Trevino. Though as far as the leaders were concerned the second day belonged to Trevino who had a 67, Watson played the first nine in one under par and held that position on the second half to finish with a 70. On the third day conditions were about as easy as they can be for scoring at Muirfield: no wind to speak of and the greens holding. Aoki beat the course record that had been set the day before by Horacio Carbonetti by one shot with a 63 and Hubert Green came in with a 64. But Watson, alone of the leaders, proved able to profit fully from the conditions and put himself securely into the lead with what he called the best round he had yet played in a major championship, 64. There is little to say about the last day. For not a moment did anyone threaten Watson in the freshening winds and Tom's 69 was almost error-free. Seldom has a champion playing his last round looked more untroubled and showed his diplomacy when he was interviewed after it was all over by declining to place the blame for the slowness of the leading pair's final round on Ken Brown, already fined during the season for slow play but apparently not a whit abashed by the experience. The pair had lost three holes on the next pairing, Trevino and Crenshaw, yet Watson plays as quickly as anyone.

Tom, however, still has something left to prove. So far we can say that no one in recent years has shown more mastery in playing on the British linksland course and that his sustained achievements on the US tournament circuit have been rivalled by few — Nicklaus, Palmer, Hogan, Snead and Nelson are the only men I would care to name. But, like Snead, the US Open still eludes him. He has threatened to win it but that is all and similarly he has no US PGA victory to his credit and but two Masters. But Tom became a golfer to reckon with as soon as he joined the US tour and his progress has been unimpeded by loss of form ever since; in fact he has dominated more as year succeeds year. Provided that the US Open does not become a psychological barrier there seems no other reason why, at thirty years of age, he should not win it a few times before he is done and by the end of the 1980s perhaps Harry Vardon's record of six victories in the British Open will be beaten.

(*left*) The most likely candidate for greatness amongst present British golfers, Sandy Lyle. There's power in reserve. I like this impact position, relaxed and everything is right (*Peter Dazeley Photography*); (*right*) Greg Norman, who has an impressive record on the European circuit and in 1981 set out to try his luck in the US (*Peter Dazeley Photography*)

Tom Watson's game is difficult to flaw in any of the departments I wrote about earlier. His driving is normally long and straight and his fellow professionals rate him as among the best of fairway wood players. Nor does he lag behind with the irons. But to me he excels most of all in the short game. He coasts the short pitches, chips and long putts close to the hole and once he is within a few feet his holing-out is near infallible.

Yet partly because of Tom's dominance, interest in the US tour has declined for it seems he lacks the indefinable charisma of a Palmer or Nicklaus, who kept the TV ratings up for so long. Our final present candidate for Mr Superman certainly does not: Severiano Ballesteros. He has just about all the ingredients you would want for the role. First there is the full, free, lashing swing that sends the ball 300 yards and more, not infrequently into wild country. Recall how the crowds warmed to Hagen and Palmer: it is easier to identify with the man who, like you, is often in the rough than the machine who is always 250 yards down the middle and has the next one on the green. In the 1920s they used to relish Hagen recovery shots far more than they did his frequent immaculate play and you could always depend on it that Walter would hit two or three shots a round that the handicap golfer would be ashamed of. Palmer's powers of recovery were even more remarkable because of the strength of those brutal hands and forearms. I'm not at all sure that the most fitting memorial to the man will not be that plaque at Royal Birkdale which commemorates a bush that received the great man's violent attentions. Though Sevvy does not have the animal force of Palmer, he perhaps has more clubhead speed and can slash the ball out of impossible places with equal panache. His victory in the 1979 British Open will, I am sure go into legend mainly because he missed the fairway time and time again but after a recovery shot was as often as not putting for a birdie.

Undoubtedly though, it is too early to evaluate this young Spaniard. Already he has curtailed his backswing and was shortly afterwards rewarded with his 1980 Masters victory. How essential an ingredient is boldness to his character I wonder? I think Palmer began to fade as caution crept into his play and the same thing could happen to Sevvy. He has already made a fortune out of the game and there have been others before him whose appetite has lessened as the bank account became fatter. To be Mr Superman you have to have passion to be the best in the world as Jones, Nelson, Hogan, Palmer, Player, Nicklaus and Watson. To know whether Ballesteros will follow these great names we must wait to see what the next few years bring and how his back stands up to the strain.

Who knows, maybe even now the world's greatest Superman Golfer is out there somewhere, practising till dusk in America, Mexico, Spain or even in Great Britain. Australia is due for another great. You can talk into the late hours, and until your hair turns silver, but some suspect there will never be anyone to equal Nicklaus, Jones, Hogan and — well, you name your own choice.

It's in the mind

I take the view that the game of golf is very largely mental, for the actual hitting of a golf ball takes so little time. The Jack Nicklaus swing, for instance, from takeaway to impact, has been timed at $1 \cdot 96$ seconds. In a long shot the ball flies for about six seconds and in all Jack hits it various distances about seventy times in an average round.

The actual performance of the golf swing itself then, for an entire round, takes only something like a couple of minutes. For the rest of the time Jack is walking, thinking, marking his partner's card maybe checking yardages and — thinking. So it's mental!

Nerves also play a huge part and some athletes take drugs to beat this — even the hearts of club players race during the monthly medal.

But don't go away saying Alliss is recommending slow-you-down drugs. I know how drugs can wreck athletes so I would recommend neither stimulants, nor depressants to my worst enemy.

I have seen some famous golfers deep in an armchair before tee-off time, yellow with strain and clearly quite ill. The stress gets to the tummy and that is why top golfers, who have to withstand strain, are worth every penny they earn. You may say you don't see many hospital cases among former golf stars, but consider the ones who suddenly fade away and are heard of no more. Do you think they woke up one day and found their swing gone? There is another factor and in my view it is the stomach. In the 1934 Open at Sandwich, Henry Cotton began 67, 65, 72 — phenomenal scoring then and remarkable even today — and this set him off on the final decisive round with a lead of no less than nine shots. While Cotton waited to tee off he was struck by what he later described as 'a terrible stomach cramp'. After the brilliance that had gone before he went out in 40 (and there were three

Henry Cotton at Royal Mid-Surrey in 1935

short holes in that half) and set off home with three 5s in a row. On the 13th, he holed a useful putt for a 4, relaxed and came back in level par to win comfortably. Henry himself is certain that the cramp had nothing to do with what he had eaten for lunch but nerves alone.

More often, however, those that fade away from public sight are not literally suffering from stomach ache. It is putting nerve that seems to go though, less frequently, the player becomes frightened to swing freely.

Some of the acknowledged great putters have been affected in this way. In his later years Vardon could only stab hopelessly at short putts. Walter Hagen, who probably had the best short game of them all in the 1920s was reduced to impotence on the greens by the late 1930s and even practised his long game assiduously, something he had disdained to do at his peak. Craig Wood, winner of both the US Masters and US Open in 1941 was later observed in an exhibition game to play his shots through the green and, once there, he picked up with his companions allowing him to credit himself with being down in two putts per green. The truth of the matter was that Craig by that time did not wish to make an exhibition of himself because of his nervous jerks and twitches at the ball. Roberto de Vicenzo, playing in the 1953 Open was tied with Hogan on 214 after the third round. In his hotel room between rounds he broke down in tears: he just knew his putting was about to let him down. Hogan finished the winner five shots ahead of Roberto. This was Hogan's last win in a major championship. Nicknamed 'The Ice Man' because of his reputation for unshakeable nerve, he was acknowledged as the best golfer in the world between tee and green until about 1960, but his putting nerve had long gone. On one occasion, faced with a crucial putt, he wandered to the edge of the green and carried out an abnormal number of practice putting strokes. He eventually returned to his ball and missed the putt. What had Hogan been doing? He later admitted that he had been trying out a number of methods in the hope of finding one that gave a remote promise of his striking the ball into the hole. His contemporary Sam Snead was a similar but more fortunate case. Sam did not adopt his between-the-legs croquet technique because he thought it was a splendid method. Sam had merely found a way that stopped him jerking at the short putts. The man blessed with arguably the smoothest swing ever seen on a golf course had become unable to move a putterhead back smoothly a foot or so and gently bring it back into contact with the ball. Then they outlawed that style.

Well I've mentioned some of the very greatest names in golf and I begin to feel that I could make out a case that *all* tournament players, lose their nerve or stomach on the greens eventually. But two names stop me: Player and Nicklaus. After twenty years and more of superstardom Player sank

(*left*) Robert de Vicenzo and I would have done better had our putting matched our long game (*Peter Dazeley Photography*); (*right*) Lee Trevino makes three or four wrongs in his swing add up to a right in the hitting area (*Peter Dazeley Photography*)

putt after putt to come from behind to win the 1978 US Masters while Jack, said to be in sharp and final decline, retorted with a couple more majors under his belt in the 1980 season.

I realise that quite a few club golfers among my readers will have been raising their eyebrows in disbelief at much of what I have had to say about panic on the greens amongst the mighty. I believe that for competent club golfers the problems are different. I've seen not a few seventy-year-olds knocking them in with never a twitch and most become better rather than worse putters the longer they have played golf. No, handicap golfers of the world, it is the longer shots that frighten you isn't it? You may have been driving very respectably throughout your round and then you are faced with a tee shot that demands avoiding a stream on the left and an out of bounds on the right. Do you swing as smoothly back as before and accelerate crisply into your drive? Or does your backswing not get much further back than your knees, followed by a quick shove at the ball, with the head lifting up before the hit to see what horrors you've perpetrated. If so, you have experienced much the same kind of panic as the tournament pro when he twitches at a putt.

So don't dismiss the mental side when assessing a golfer. The winners are the best thinkers and know how to handle themselves under duress, and know what to eat and say, and what not to eat — and not to say. A cutting remark can hurt someone else, and unsettle your own poise.

I would like to be able to help golfers to think their way round to a better score and frankly, this is possible. So many people don't really believe in themselves and my father Percy Alliss used to be able to spot possible winners just by talking with them.

There is no other game in this world that requires greater restraint of feelings. There are so many petty things which can annoy the golfer, and put him off his game but if he has the right spirit, no irritation can deter him. Outstanding examples of cool ones are Bobby Locke, Walter Hagen, Peter Thomson and Ben Hogan. Club-throwers don't often win, although there have been exceptions such as Norman von Nida of Australia and Tommy Bolt of America. And Scotland's Eric Brown wasn't always sweetness and light on or off the course.

Golf reveals character and sometimes the most cheerful and good-humoured fellow will become sullen, nervous or unapproachable when he is playing in a competition he regards as important. The girls, too, take the game seriously, as indeed they should, but look out for the ones with dry lips and a strained expression; they may 'blow-up' when the pressure gets fierce!

My father used to reckon that when two players are going round together, either as partners or rivals, they are bound to influence each other in some way. The more highly strung one may be more susceptible to the other's play. I have seen this happen more than once. Take a top golfer such as Lee Trevino who likes to chatter away and crack jokes with spectators. Put him with a quiet introverted type of competitor, Neil Coles perhaps, and you may have a problem. The gallery like the jokes, but your introvert wants none of it. I sometimes think those who decide which players to put together for a big event such as the Open, might bear these things in mind because if they are just drawn by chance you can end up with some unfortunate incidents.

If you are playing with a nervous person, it is sometimes a good idea to try to ignore him totally. Try not to become caught up in their mindless chatter, often indulged in because of nerves alone.

Now suppose you are drawn to play with a quick player. In this case my advice is to try not to watch him play the first few shots. He may influence you in some awful way. On the other hand, I remember the Oxford and Cambridge teams always used to enjoy playing with that fine old amateur Leonard Crawley, who had about him the easy rhythm of a champion. His swing was delightfully slow and the young lads thought they might catch his rhythm — and play a blinder. Some of them did.

In match-play it is a good idea to think just of your own game and not to continually watch your rival's doings in the hope of a mistake which will let you in. The dangerous time in any match is the first half an hour or hour. You haven't quite got into the thing and if a rival upsets you in some way, the influence is obviously bad. Also, if an opponent seems off his game and mutters angrily, take no notice and concentrate just as hard on your own shot. Don't let up because you think he's playing like an idiot because he could just drag you down to his level and your pars will soon become his bogeys.

One of the curious things about golf matches is that people so often sink to the level of a partner, or an opponent. They think they have the match in hand, slump to a couple of 5s at par 4 holes and then, to their dismay, find their opponent suddenly hit a purple patch and win a match that should have been lost.

My father said he made it a rule never to play slackly however bad the company. If he was two or three up he would concentrate on winning the next hole, and the next. The trick is to try to attain your own highest standard, irrespective of what is happening to a rival, or a partner. Watching what the other fellow does is a recipe for defeat.

Probably you've noticed how something unexpected can swing a whole match. Maybe you are two down and heading for defeat. Suddenly you hit a particularly good pitch shot which takes a lucky bounce, and rolls into the hole. Bingo. Your opponent is rattled, thinks you are enjoying a smile from God, and goes to pieces. A hole he thought he was going to win, he loses — taking three putts. You remember it happening in the 1972 Open at Muirfield when Trevino holed a chip shot at the 71st hole and Britain's hope, Tony Jacklin three-putted and lost the Open. It happens every day, somewhere.

A good rule is to play every shot with the intention of bringing off a miracle shot. After all, the others chip it in — so why not you? And they seem to hole their share of long putts. Everyone does. So can you and you will be more likely to if you are really trying to do so.

We all know the type who is put off by a dog or a train. Ignore his complaints and never, ever, make excuses for yourself. My father used to say the patron saint of these irritable individuals was a cantankerous colonel advancing, purple-faced and murderous, upon an unfortunate caddie who had dared to move an eyelid. There was even an old-time cartoon on this. But such golfers exist today and one, fairly recently in America, was said to have done to death a goose which honked as he was about to putt. He denied all this but the case went to court and much heated argument ensued.

I'm always astonished how quiet, reasonable people lose their calmness when they take to the course. But the secret of low scores is a low temperature and I'm sure failings of temperament can be conquered just like the great Bobby Jones showed after his first visit to St Andrews in 1921. He went out in the high 40s, then took two shots to get out of a bunker and tore his card to pieces. Indeed as a young player Jones was just about infamous for his fiery temper and a bad shot usually was followed by a flung club. The St Andrews incident, Jones said, caused him to mend his ways. He continued to suffer from nerves, being unable to eat before playing and losing several pounds in weight during a tournament, but he never let his anger show. In his great years from 1923 to his retirement at twenty-eight in 1930 he is not reported to have thrown a club or stamped his foot again. Instead he became the epitome of the way a golfer should comport himself. Perhaps his nearest equivalents today are Watson, Crenshaw, Trevino and Nicklaus. How much better it is to see your favourite shake his head ruefully in self-criticism than fling a club to (at?) his caddie or lash it into the ground.

Jones did not love St Andrews after that first visit but later he came back to love it, and the golf course responded by allowing him to win there.

I've always believed you should 'make friends' with a course. It is no use complaining that the fairways are rough, or the whole place should be towed out to sea, and sunk. Learn to appreciate it, and maybe bring it to its knees.

Golf is a thinking person's game. Never forget it.

Just to prove the point that your mind dictates, that great teacher Bill Cox, a past Ryder Cup player, once almost cured a pupil with a chronic hook. He told him to shut the face at address. The young man looked up, shocked. 'If I do that I'll kill somebody' he stuttered. But Bill insisted — and the penny dropped. The wild hooker realised that unless he brought the clubface into the ball square, he probably would do some damage, and would certainly lose a ball. 'The hands do it all', said Bill. And he's right there!

The Americans are great thinkers at golf. Lee Trevino talks about his 'game plan' and Jack Nicklaus paces off the yards. He knows how many yards he hits each club — do you? Not easy to do but you can get some idea of your power. But remember that Nicklaus is a consistent striker. If he hits an 8-iron 150 yards he will only vary a few yards either side of that distance.

Hubert Green goes down the shaft for most of his shots. The second frame shows how he 'lifts' the club away from the ball and later loops it round (*Peter Dazeley Photography*)

98

Even so, the top players say that they hit a perfect shot little more than once a round. Test yourself this way. Decide what distance you think you hit a particular club — say a 7-iron. Now go out and hit a dozen shots on your practice ground. Discount the one you topped and the one you hit rather heavily. Also discount the two that whistled out of the middle of the club face. None of those shots, either the bad or the good, are near your average length. Those remaining eight, the ones you hit moderately crisply, will give you a reasonable idea of the distance you can expect to hit a 7-iron. You are now equipped to avoid one of the errors that a handicap golfer makes; he over estimates the distance he can hit each and every one of his irons. This is specially so in playing par 3s when there is a yardage inscribed on the tee marker which so often causes him to insist to himself that his 'normal' length with a 9-iron is, say, 130 yards when 110 is probably far nearer the mark. But what, you may ask, if I do hit a good one? I'll be through the green. True and here you should briefly weigh up the odds. But if you doubt the wisdom of what I've been saying test me out the next time you are out in a four-ball. Count up how many approach shots (it applies to chips and the little pitches too to some extent) are short of the flag and how many are too long. I would bet that the proportion would be about 10:1.

Most people have to concentrate to score well. Those who apply themselves and concentrate on their own game can sometimes beat rivals of greater talent who, maybe, have a poor mental attitude. We all know about top players who don't recognise their wives in the gallery. It's called the 'What train?' mentality after the story of a train which roared past the great Joyce Wethered as she putted. 'Didn't that train upset you?' they asked, amazed she had holed an awkward putt. Her reply proved she had been concentrating: 'What train?'

Concentrate a little harder on the closing holes, even if you have just scored a birdie. I've seen even Nicklaus quicken his pace after knocking in a long putt. But he steadies down before the next drive, and gets his mind working again. In other words, put the last hole behind you, whether you birdied or bogeyed it.

Another good idea is to think how your best shot will look before you hit it. Imagine you see it flying and shape the shot in your head before you even stand to the ball. It helps because you are thinking positively, of a successful shot, perhaps soaring high and straight and then drifting right or left before plummeting down at the flag. If, however, you just swing hopefully with no such image and very little at all in mind then the shot will quite likely match your vagueness of purpose. Worse, if you are frightened of what's about to happen, your shot will lack conviction and you are likely to lift up on the shot in your anxiety to see which patch of bushes or bunker your ball is hopping towards. Bobby Locke, for instance, concentrated on slowness *before* he arrived at the course. He said that he even shaved slowly! All this was to try to achieve a state of measured relaxation and to deal with tension. Once he was playing he moved along a golf course not so much slowly as unhurriedly. Some claimed indeed that he played far too slowly but I don't think that this was true. Once at his ball, for instance, Locke took very little time to play. He had already decided how to play the shot and he then took up his stance, a couple of practice swings to get the 'feel' of the shot and away it went. (Compare this with one of today's superstars, Hubert Green. I'm always meaning to count up how many times he taps his club to the ground behind his ball and looks up to the target but it must be more than a dozen. Hubert is a very tense player, and no doubt this is his way of coping with that tension: he doesn't hit the ball until he is confident that everything is in order.)

Notice how most good golfers have a pattern, especially for the longer shots. We all know how Nicklaus lines up at an insignificant target a couple of feet from his ball and, just before he swings, turns his head to the right. Some (Howard Clark, for instance) pull at their clothing as if to ensure that it is loose; others hitch up their trousers (Palmer); some shrug their shoulders to check that the shirt isn't sticking. These are mostly nervous habits but they do serve to reassure the player that all is well. Better to have a particular drill that is never changed, however important the shot: if you normally take one light practice swing, don't change to two because you *must* get this one on the green or lose the match. Above all, do not take longer the more important a shot is; it will only result in increased tension. Mind you the joker who throws up grass cuttings into the air and said he didn't know why he was doing it, except he'd seen Palmer doing it, was probably only holding up play — but yes, find where the wind is coming from without using a dirty handkerchief!

The pre-shot pattern matters. So does positive thinking as Gary Player will tell you. If you don't believe in yourself, and the shot you are about to play, nobody else will. Another tip. Don't lose your temper. I know Dai Rees once said his doctor had told him it would damage his health if he bottled up his emotions, but that doesn't mean you should sling your favourite driver because you might crack its neck. And then what?

Try to play a lot of your golf under pressure. That might mean friendly games for a side bet. A little wager adds spice to the meal. Trevino said 'playing for five dollars when you only have three' is real pressure.

They say taking deep breaths helps relax you. I've even read that when the heat is really on you should think only of slowing down the backswing. One chap even advised that we shouldn't ever clench our fists on a golf course as it built tension.

The Casper method

If you wanted to talk with a good professional who had made some really good spending money in the last few years, you would have about a hundred to choose from. That is the total number of professional golfers in this world who really make their skill or knowledge pay off significantly. This is not to say there aren't hundreds more who pay their grocery bills from enterprises connected with golf, but I'm talking about players who can honestly place their hand on their heart and say they have been a success.

One of them, in a quiet way, is an American called Billy Casper. He's off the circuit now, but he made a million and if he hadn't been a success at golf, he looks as if he might have become a bank manager. If you saw him on a train, you wouldn't suspect he was a big-winning athlete. So let's finally hear from him in a tape-recorded piece.

Billy Casper won more than a million dollars, though sadly a few bad deals have cost him almost the lot, as well as the United States Opens of

1959 and 1966. He made the game look simple and was a magnificent putter. One day he agreed to record his thoughts on how to play golf. What he said was memorable.

The driver is the most important club in the bag because it sets the hole up. If you hit a good one, you have more or less taken care of fifty per cent of the problem on each hole, so it is important people spend a lot of time learning to drive and keeping the ball in play.

In my style I use a slightly closed stance with the feet no wider than my shoulders. The weight is evenly distributed, not back on the heels or up on the toes, but firmly planted on the soles of the feet. By closed stance I mean this: If you draw an imaginary line in the direction that you wish to hit the ball, your right foot would be withdrawn off this line just about an inch or so.

If you watch professionals play, you'll see they have different characteristics or different fundamentals in taking the club away, and arriving at the top of the swing. But on the downswing from about waist-height, right into the hitting zone, their fundamentals are all the same. It is important a player perfects his fundamentals, or characteristics, to the best of his ability — and plays with them.

When I first joined the tour I was a chronic hooker. I used to hit the ball low with a very fast backswing. I used a closed stance, aimed one way, and hit it another. I worked very hard trying to correct this, opened up my stance a little bit but this resulted in fading the ball. I used to play to the left side of the fairway and let it fade to the right centre.

I'm still a firm believer that a good player must either hook the ball, or fade it. By playing one way or another you eliminate half the troubles that exist on each hole. If you hit the ball right to left, you eliminate all the trouble on the right of the fairway and all you need think about is drawing the ball into the left or centre of the fairway. By the same token, if you fade, you eliminate problems on the left side.

The toughest shot in the game is the straight one because it takes a perfect swing to hit it straight. I believe you must play this game by using the percentages. By consistently either fading or drawing the ball a golfer hits more fairways and has a finer chance of a lower score.

Many people have the wrong concept of golf. They think of it as a game of brute force. In fact it is one of timing and co-ordination and course management: being able to think out your shot; where you want to place it.

I use the conventional overlapping grip and hold the club firmly with the left hand because, at the top of the swing, if I didn't hold on, the weight of the club would force the last three fingers to open. Then I'd have to regrip and I would lose all the power I generate with a wristcock.

I have a little stronger left-hand grip than some. I may show two and a half knuckles. The right hand grips the club more in the fingers, for the right is the hand that has the power in the golf swing. The left hand and side are the control side. It is important you hold the club firmly with the right because this is the hand with the power. Do not grip tightly as you tighten up the tendons and muscles in the forearm as this restricts free movement of the golf swing. The game should be played in a relaxed frame of mind and if you get headaches and ulcers from your golf, why turn professional!

(*above*) Castletown, Isle of Man — the 17th hole, 'The Gully', during the PGA Cup Match in 1979, British Isles v USA, won by the home team (*Bert Neale*); (*below*) Royal St Davids, Harlech — the 2nd hole with the imposing Harlech Castle in the background (*Bert Neale*)

(*above*) Sotogrande, Spain — the 15th green (*Bert Neale*); (*below*) Penina, Portugal — looking across the 18th fairway towards the hotel (*Bert Neale*)

Think about how you pick up an egg. You grip it tight enough so you don't break the shell, firm enough so you don't drop it.Though Arnold Palmer does not do this. When he grips a golf club he leaves finger imprints in the grip. But he had great results so that's why I say there is no set way of playing. But you must do some of the things certain players do, then if they work, stick with them. If they don't, dismiss them.

If you read books and take lessons you will find one person will contradict another, or a player will even contradict himself. It depends on what phase he is going through at the time. I believe if something works for you, stay with it.

It's important that the hands work together. Actually the best way would be to sew your hands together. You can't do this, but try to get as near as possible to it. Take care not to get the right hand under the shaft because then you'll really turn it over and smother shots.

When I drive I tee the ball up forward in my stance, opposite about the middle of the instep of my left foot. This is more forward than most players. With the driver you're catching the ball slightly on the upswing.

The back of the left hand is the most important thing in a golf swing because it is going to control where the ball goes. I find the longer I can keep the back of this hand moving at my target, quite often the straighter I'll hit the ball. If I allow the left hand to collapse and roll over, it means a hook. If I keep the left hand moving too fast out, and way to the outside, I'll hit the ball to the right. I relate the back of the left hand to the clubface.

Think of it this way. When you put the club on the ground, the back of the left hand and the face of the club are one and the same. For whatever you do with the left hand, you're going to do with the clubface.

The right hand is the one that adds power. If you find you continually hit it heavy it's because you're quitting with the left hand and your right hand takes over and causes you to hit behind the ball. You're using too much right, and not keeping the left moving through the ball.

Remember a closed stance is a power stance. When you are striving for distance, this is the type to use. It enables you to turn away from the ball better, and turn back on it. It will cause you to generate a bigger arc and this is where you gain power. Mind you, don't try to overpower the ball and swing well within yourself at all times.

Where the toes point, is something you should work out on the practice area. Your weight should be evenly distributed so if you're playing in a strong wind it doesn't make you move. Your hips, shoulders, hands and feet all line up on the target and if they do not, it's pretty tough to get the ball to go where you're aiming. If your shoulders are aiming at a different place from your hips and your feet there is no way to hit the ball straight. So everything has to aim at the target.

I find it is most important for me to find an object to shoot at so I can draw a line on it. Whatever club I'm using, this is important. Whether it's a flagstick, a sand trap or a tree, just something I can draw a bead on. Maybe if you are going to draw the ball, aim a little to the right of it, and work it back.

It's important when you prepare to hit a shot that you use a waggle, move your feet, keep them in the same position, but regripping the ground and maybe start your swing with a forward press.

I've only known one player who started his swing from a dead stop — Doug

105

Casper aims at a target (*Peter Dazeley Photography*)

Sanders — and he can swing in a telephone booth! Most players have something in movement as they prepare to hit each shot, and this breaks up tension. So go right ahead and waggle; it relaxes you and helps a smooth and free swing. Sanders is unique with his swing because if you watch all the fine players, you'll never see any of them come from a dead start.

I try to take the club back square, keeping the blade square to the intended line. This is the way I play because I use a slightly upright swing. Playing the ball more forward in my stance enables me to swing more upright. I take it back to the waist before the wrist cock starts. From there they cock until the top of the swing. I do not overswing as this can set up possible errors. The club should never go past parallel to the ground at the top.

Incidentally, it is a misconception that the left arm is straight. The only fellow with a straight left arm is Sam Snead and that is because he was born double-jointed. So the left arm should be kept firm, but not rigid and straight. There is a slight bend in the left arm at the top and if you look at all players, you can see it.

The toughest thing we humans have to do with each other here upon the earth is to communicate. So when I say I take the club straight back from the ball I mean until about waist high, keeping the blade square. And I mean without taking it on the outside that way, and without any rolling. The left heel comes off the ground and when you're at the top, the left arm has a slight break. Once you develop this kind of swing, it really is most simple.

Eliminate any superflous movement, straight back and up over your head does sound simple. Everything works together going back. The head remains right over the ball and if it moves the upper part of the body moves back with it and then you're in a bad position at the top and the only thing you can do is lunge forward and you have created two wrongs which cannot make one right. So keep your head plumb centre, pivot and your weight is on your right foot at the top, your head directly over the ball, your weight stays on the axle which is your backbone and your weight just swivels around it.

Keep that axle firm right over the ball. Your weight stays on the inside of your feet — if it ever gets to the outside you are going to sway.

One of the most common faults at the top of the swing of a person who slices is a poor position. He tries to hit it hard and throws the clubface into the ball from the outside. He leaves the blade open, comes across the ball, and hits a slice. If he does this, but manages to close the face as he comes down, the result is a hook or pull.

If I'm going to intentionally hook the ball I hit it a little from the inside, but to deliberately slice finds me hitting it a little bit from outside. I very, very seldom change my grip for these shots; I do it with my swing.

There are no short cuts to good golf, but only through sheer work and practice can you develop a good game. You ask about golfers who move their left side into the ball. This way you are either going to flat hook, or knock it to the right. I hit into a firm left side, and let her go, under it. The trouble with a slicer is he gets too quick and forgets about keeping his movement, and everything goes.

Golf is the toughest game ever invented. In every other sport there's sudden movement and your reflexes take over. In golf, the ball is there, here's the club, now you produce the movement and get it over there and into a little hole. And the winds are blowing at you as well.

In golf, everything works sideways and under. We are going against all the muscle training we have done, all our lives. In golf we have to get into an awkward position and it really is an unnatural thing to drive a golf ball.

I can't stress how important the left hand is in a golf swing. It keeps you moving through the ball and somewhere after you have hit the ball, the right hand catches up and turns the club over. But it shouldn't happen until after you make contact. The pros may all work a little bit different but the left hand is the important one and that's a reason why Ben Hogan, who was originally left-handed, made such a great golfer.

I do no exercises whatever. As I got a little older I thought about it but I didn't want to lose what I had. I found fishing and pool complemented my golf because they are touch things, like golf. I'll stay with what I have, stay with the upright swing. Most of the good players have an upright swing. Tony Lema had a wonderful swing and with this method you have very little hip pronation, I guess you would call it. Upright means you don't have to rely so much on rolling your hips.

People sometimes ask how many perfect shots I hit in a round. I tell them about half a dozen, as planned but when you think about it if you really do hit six perfect shots on eighteen holes, you've had an exceptional round!

2
Knowing the the Rules

Henry Longhurst once argued that the rules of golf should be written on the back of a cigarette packet, in fairly large handwriting. In a perfect world, a bold statement like that would be proved correct but, alas, things have not quite worked out that way.

However, some rules are more abused than others and, quite often, they are the simple ones: the basic ones we really ought to know, but don't.

Let's talk about some of the essential things you should know, always bearing in mind what Henry was really driving at: that if you are an honest, upright gentleman you shouldn't need to be told that you don't crush a newly planted tree to death in order to get at your ball; or tee up in the rough just because your opponent isn't looking!

We've all seen the petty cheat. He presses his foot behind his ball so it sits up asking to be hit; he drops his clubs with a clatter when you are halfway back with your driver; he allows his shadow to fall across your ball at the vital moment; he rattles coins, chatters stupidly and is generally not ever again worth playing with. So don't.

Before I tackle the simple parts of the rules, I'd like to dig deeply into this aspect of golf, starting with the background to some big-time incidents which led to heavy fines being imposed on really good players who should have known better, from the standpoint of behaviour, and continuing to basic cheating, which has gone on, I suppose, since the dawn of golf.

Legal papers have come into my hands which show that today, more then ever, professional golfers are in need of legal advice owing to the enormous financial inducements and awards for top players. Substantial sums of money are at stake in the major events and a hasty or wrong decision by a competitor regarding the interpretation of a rule could cost him not only a title, but the additional income created by his status as champion.

As far as I can judge from the rules of golf, there is nothing there to say a competitor shall not take a legal adviser round with him to interpret the rules of golf which, in all conscience, are complicated enough to warrant this.

Problems with golf law go back at least as far as 1632 when a group of men played in, of all places, the local kirkyard in Kelso. Unluckily one of the spectators was struck on the head and died soon afterwards. The father of the deceased started criminal proceedings. All the players were blamed for the slaughter of the dead person 'by giving hame ane dedlie straik with ane golf ball under his left lug at golf in the kirk yaird'. The case was eventually abandoned as it was said nobody could be certain who had struck the fatal shot.

The question of when an amateur may or may not accept payment towards his expenses incurred in competing can also give rise to problems of legal interpretation. The player may well have some difficulty in satisfying both the Inland Revenue and the Rules Committee of the R and A at the same time.

The rule relating to amateur status says it is permissible to play in competition while on an expenses-paid business trip, providing the golf part of the expenses is borne personally and is not charged to business. In addition, it is said the business must be actual and substantial and not merely a subterfuge for legitimising expenses.

And there's more. Joining a golf club in the furtherance of business interests is not a deductible expense. Also, I understand that any professional seeking to regain his amateur status must fill in a special form — and drafting such applications could involve considerable legal skills not always present in sportspeople who have spent most of their time hitting golf balls!

In America the increasing use of power-driven buggies has led to court cases. A number of players have been seriously injured in accidents and huge damages have been awarded. A New York attorney claims that golf carts are rarely given the service and maintenance they require and no licence or test is required to drive one which leads, inevitably, to all kinds of pile-ups and cries from those who want to see a 'Fairway Code'.

One court case centred around a lady golfer more used to playing hockey. She demonstrated the swing to her friend, swinging at a daisy. Unhappily the friend was not paying sufficient attention at the time and was firmly hit by the follow-through. She went to court where it was suggested an element of danger existed in all games which, it was said, heightened the enjoyment. Mr Justice Swift jumped in at this. He asked: 'You are not suggesting people enjoy their golf more because they may be driven into? The language one hears on golf courses does not suggest that it is a pleasurable pursuit.'

A suggestion was then put forward that the lady spoke to the imaginary ball before she started to swing. Mr Justice Swift: 'You do not speak to a ball before you drive. You are obviously thinking of addressing a jury which is one thing; addressing a ball is another.' The whole case produced not a little tittering and the outcome, I'm afraid, is shrouded in uncertainty as far as I'm concerned.

Golfers, being usually honourable men, seldom break the rules. But every year there are what the newspapers like to call 'incidents' and the 19th hole often buzzes with confusion as to what old so-and-so should have done when his ball plugged in mud, or whatever. Plugging of the ball does indeed give rise to more dispute than many other matters for it can usually be coupled with casual water. If the ground is soft enough for the ball to plug, then it is usually possible to tramp around and declare that water is appearing on the surface by your shoes. I think myself that at club level there should be a local rule in winter (summer too after heavy rain) that a ball resting in its own impression *anywhere* on the course, other than in a hazard, may be lifted and dropped. As it is, a ball may be lifted and placed usually, under winter rules and that, of course, takes care of the plugged ball but the poor fellow plugged in the rough obtains no such relief — hence the heavy trample of feet and the claims of casual water.

Again at club level, and by means again of a local rule I should be very happy to see the rule that requires the flagstick to be attended abolished or in any class of golf for that matter. What a time-waster it is and as golf gets slower and slower anything helps. What so often happens is that one player puts his shot to the green at the front, with the flag at the back. He then has to wait until one of the other three trundle their trolleys round the green and one of them becomes available to attend the flag. Often at least a couple of minutes pass before this happens. In the meantime our first player could have made his approach putt and be at the flag ready for the next to putt. Shorter, but still useful, savings of time would also result when no one is particularly far from the flag.

Of course, it will be said that it is an advantage to putt with the flagstick in; that when a putt is charged, the ball can clatter into the flag and stop dead or even down the hole. True, this would happen from time to time but there are disadvantages too in striking the flag. If your ball strikes it just off centre, the rebound will always be further than if it had struck the softer earth of the hole itself.

Even the stars find themselves in the headlines over the rules. Who can forget how upset Jack Nicklaus was following the Wentworth affair in the 1966 Piccadilly World Match-Play when he was not allowed to pick up his ball because his claim that a cigarette advertisement was in his line of sight was not accepted by Colonel Tony Duncan.

111

If you don't recognise him, the name's on the bag (*Peter Dazeley Photography*)

On the special rule sheet that day was the 'line of sight' rule, which is used in all events these days where TV towers, stands and so on may obstruct the line to the flagstick. It read clearly enough: 'Temporary towers and trucks for TV, broadcasting and photography, tents, scoreboards, temporary refreshment stands, parked cars, canvas screen and scaffolding are to be treated as immovable objects . . . and the ball may be lifted without penalty and dropped at the nearest point where there is no intervention, and must come to rest not nearer the hole than its original position.'

Duncan, the referee, abdicated after a difference of opinion with Nicklaus, who had been caught in a ditch, picked and dropped, and then apparently found the cigarette advertisement in his way. Another version, however, was that his ball had fallen into an awful place, but memory fades, and frankly some cannot even remember who Jack was playing. But an incident it undoubtedly was!

The referee who took over was Gerald Micklem, a rules expert. He said many people in Britain view the rules differently from Americans in general, and American tournament players in particular, and that is obviously true. In Britain, he said, we tend to play the rules honourably and more to their spirit. We do not always take full advantage of our rights and in all classes of golf are equally lax in our application of penalties, said Micklem, with some regret.

But Micklem put his finger on the essential point where he maintained that though in America they play the rules honestly they demand that everything be written down clearly in black and white. If this is done they then accept all the penalties — and see that everyone else does so, too. But, says Micklem, they also demand their rights in full as well. For the American tournament player, the rule book is his Bill of Rights.

'With the money at stake', wrote Micklem at the time, 'I feel there is a lot to be said for their way, but it does mean they will make a lot of claims of which we would not approve in our honourable way. I do not say for sure that it was the case in this instance; but if any part of that billboard or its support did intervene between the ball and the hole, then Jack felt he was entitled to a drop, even if only to try to get a better lie. We of our generation may not like this spirit but it is a fact and we should be prepared to accept it.' So the Jack Nicklaus affair was laid to rest, although even today golfers still talk about it, year after year, with all kinds of very similar incidents which the World Match-Play championships at Wentworth throw up.

Disputes involving tournament players and the mistakes of interpretation they make are always good for coverage in the media. Take the Weiskopf incident on the US circuit a few seasons ago. Tom was short of the green, wanted to look at all the ground up to the flag, and was not in a sunny mood. On his route lay a bunker. Instead of walking round, Tom impatiently strode through the middle of it. Some esoteric discussion followed this. If Tom had then hit his approach into the bunker what would the ruling have been? Could it have been decided that he had deliberately 'improved' his lie before playing the shot even if his ball had finished in a heel mark which Tom himself had made? Well it would have been a titillating matter but, alas, Tom did not then finish in the bunker and no decision was called for.

Or let us consider altering the playing characteristics of clubs. I suspect, to the considerable woe of manufacturers, and my own contract with one of them, that it is technically entirely feasible to produce an iron adjustable for loft and weight of clubhead, supplied with a telescopic shaft to take care of length of shaft. You would then be equipped with everything between a 1-iron and pitching wedge with a putter thrown in for good measure (alas no sand wedge though it might just be possible to slot a flange into the sole of the club). A few balls and some tee pegs in the pocket and you are all set to stroll round your course idly flicking at the daisies of a summer's evening or hunched with hands in pockets on a frosty, gusty winter's morning. But, you say, what about my driver? No great problems. I expect we could give you a screw-on wood head to put in the other pocket. Well the Japanese did produce something along these lines and off it went to the R and A for the seal of official approval. Alas, it did not get that approval for it offended the rule which declares that a golfer must not alter the 'playing characteristics' of a club during play.

Which, in a fairly trivial way, is what Sandy Lyle did while playing in a

(*left*) Nick Faldo (*Peter Dazeley Photography*); (*right*) Tom Watson prepares for the 1978 Open at St Andrews. Tom Kite is on his left (*Michael Hobbs*)

tournament early in the 1980 season. It was sunny and Sandy found himself being dazzled by his putterhead so he stuck some tape over the offending reflection. Nick Faldo felt that this broke the rule we have been discussing and reported Lyle, who promptly departed the tournament, disqualified. Why, you may ask, didn't Nick point out to Sandy that he was about to break the rule when he saw the tape being applied to the putter? I don't know, but it might well be that he was aware of that other rule that, under penalty of two strokes, forbids offering advice to another player. Remember Tom Watson in a 1980 US tournament? In kindly and helpful mood, he told Lee Trevino, his playing partner that round, he was playing the ball too far forward in his stance. Of course there is a difference between these two circumstances: Watson was giving advice, basically, about how to play the game; Faldo, in warning Lyle, would have been giving information about the rules of golf and this is allowed.

As all this shows, the rules of golf are both complex and subtle and are intended to cover all the circumstances that can occur. What though do you think about the following sequence of events (I'll have to be unspecific about people and places or I might find myself in court).

A and B, two local club pros were drawn together in a tournament on the 1980 European circuit. At the second hole, both drove into a fairway bunker. B made a good long recovery, getting his ball near the green. A then settled into his stance before trying to achieve a similar result, then 'This isn't my ball', he said. 'Weren't you playing a Titleist 4?' 'Yes', B replied without hesitation. 'Would you fetch my ball then please?' A asked. 'Get it yourself' was the reply. As A thought the situation was already deteriorating rapidly, he set off to retrieve his own ball without further discussion.

On his return, without speaking, he handed it to B, who walked into the sand and forced it into the face of the bunker. 'Right', he said, 'let's see you get that out!' Of course A protested that his ball had been in a clean lie on the floor of the bunker, well enough for B to have been able to move it 170 or so yards. B did not bother to deny this, and was content to say that it was up to him to rule where the ball had been.

As they were two unknowns they were playing entirely alone so it was A's word against B's and it seems that A was bashful about summoning a PGA official to give a ruling. No doubt he was also bemused — I can think of no golfer who has suffered anything remotely comparable. So he took out his sand wedge and managed to blast it out a few yards on to the fairway. History does not record whether or not the remainder of the round was played out in friendly spirit.

Countless millions of golfers bend the rules, very often because they don't

Gary Player puts everything into it (*Peter Dazeley Photography*)

know them and the worst offenders, very often, are we the British! I can recall the hue and cry when Gary Player hit a backhanded shot with his putter in a match against Arnold Palmer. He was obliged to play some kind of left-handed shot and the back of his putter had an odd line to it and certainly would not have conformed to the rules as regards the shape of a club *face*.

Another incident that concerned Player occurred at the 1974 Open at Royal Lytham and St Anne's. Near the end of his final round, in a comfortable lead over his nearest rival, Peter Oosterhuis, Player lost his ball in deep rough. For a while the championship began to look more open, if Player could not find his ball and dropped two shots and if Oosterhuis could finish strongly. However, the ball was found and Player was champion. Shortly after, a club member in the same patch of rough found a ball inscribed 'Gary Player' and of the same make and number as Player had been using that day, or so it is claimed. The questions remain: was the ball Player found the correct one or another identical that, perhaps, he had lost during practice? Or is this story true at all!

So finally let's put you, the reader, to the test. I'll assume you know the rules and would not consider cheating. But have you ever used your feet to clear back some bushes before hacking out of the jungle? Have you ever trodden down a pitch mark on the green? Do you pick your ball out of a rabbit scrape if the rabbit scrape is under a bush? The rules are said to be models of clarity — but are they?

What about the lost ball? There you are, searching around in the hay for your ball — and your feet find it. You must have changed its lie to some degree. Do you then inform your opponent that you've found your ball, but accidently moved it? You should, and take the one-stroke penalty, even though it was hard luck. Considerable ill feeling was generated in one Ryder Cup when we British decided to play it tough. Eric Brown, the captain, told his team not to look for balls lost by their US opponents to avoid the risk of penalty strokes if they found them with their feet, thus unavoidably moving the ball.

Even at quite a high level of golf you will occasionally see players smoothing down the rough round their ball. They pick up the odd leaf and twig here and there — that's fine — but, in doing so, also smooth something down. Some even get their foot to that tuft of grass behind the ball, or push the turf down while addressing the ball with an iron. Then suddenly they find the lie is good enough for a 4-wood! At nearly every golf club there are two or three players who are known to cheat. They are the people who have to be clearly out of bounds or in a water hazard before they lose a ball. Otherwise, it always miraculously appears — often in a good lie — usually when the other players have given up the search and moved on. If you watch them carefully in the rough you will sooner or later see a foot come down very firmly behind the ball, notice a few practice swings that just happen to remove an awkward tuft of grass and sometimes a nudge with foot of clubhead to move the ball to a more attractive spot. And if, after all these afforts they still arrive at the green having played rather too many shots you can depend that their counting will do their score no harm at all. 'How many are you, Jack?' you ask. 'Six?' The answer will certainly be no more than five.

Probably the worst cheats cannot help themselves and certainly the attitude of their fellow players reflects this. You might expect them to be outcasts but surprisingly this is seldom the case. An amused contempt is the more usual reaction, made possible because the cheat at club golf level is nearly always a poor golfer and therefore has little influence on the average four-ball. Nevertheless, what goes on inside his head as he boasts in the bar afterwards of a par here and there and a gross score a few better than it really was?

Eric Brown

How well I remember Arthur Lees, former Ryder Cup player and then the pro at Sunningdale, shattering the cheat who liked to mark his ball on the green in order to manoeuvre it just a little nearer the hole. He'd pick the ball up, and then put the marker down. The advance had begun. He'd clean his ball, then pick up his marker. And then put down the ball, even nearer still. Arthur watched all this, then: 'No need to putt that one now. You've turned it into a bloody gimme.' But cheats don't blush, although I fancy this gentleman didn't play with Arthur again, which was his loss.

Amateurs like to think that the pros 'bend' the rules and a very good amateur friend of mine will give a demonstration concerning a world-wide golfer who found his ball too close to a stubby piece of heather for his liking. The story comes from a spectator, a young man who wanted to see how the expert coped with this. He was a steward for the day so was able to push forward for a close-up.

'Get back on the right' said the star. 'And get back on the left.' There was apparently much pacing up and down, and the golfer in question trampled the twiggy problem to death. The young steward never saw how to play the

119

Arthur Lees lining up a putt at Sunningdale shortly before his retirement in 1975: a great character and a real 'pro' (*Sporting Pictures (UK) Ltd*)

stroke. He was upset, said so, and 'Your job is to steward' he was told 'Not to spy!'

Another form of rule-bending comes under the heading of gamesmanship and most of us have been exposed to it, particularly in match-play where nerves get twisted and quite aimless wanderings can be construed as a deliberate attempt to put one off. And very little is sometimes needed to do this. Who has not heard of the character in a Wodehouse story who was unable to concentrate because of the 'uproar of butterflies' in an adjoining meadow. Or the man who complained about ships sailing past on the horizon.

Rattling the opposition can be quite subtle, far more so than rattling coins in the pocket while he's thinking of starting the backswing. I've come across those who slowly pull the velcro from the left-hand glove — it makes an almost show-biz tearing sound. Then there was the chap who liked to strike his match slowly, and the other fellow who would hit his own drive, and then start to tell a story with the punch-line held up for your drive, which was then usually hurried and without concentration.

Some over-keen types like to stand where your eye can pick them up, and if you ask them to move this probably upsets you slightly more than it does them. 'Oh, getting fussy in your old-age?' and other similar remarks are trotted out. One chap was even accused of moving his white shoes to put someone off.

Saying the wrong thing can often be close to cheating. Remarks like: 'Watch the bunker with your hook' or 'You were out of bounds here last week' produce the kind of keen resentment guaranteed to impair the most elegant backswings and the smart Alecs think themselves so clever. And yet, really cunning gamesmanship, as advocated by Stephen Potter, often bring a smile to one's face. Trouble is, once you smile at it, your concentration wanders — and he's got you again!

The game has thrown up some quite intriguing incidents in which the rules were involved. Harry Bradshaw finding his ball in the broken bottle during an Open championship at Sandwich will always be spoken about, even though it was back in 1949. Poor Harry, instead of seeking a ruling as to whether or not he could drop his ball without penalty, decided to play the ball out, smashing the pieces across the course. One shot gone, and in the end he tied Bobby Locke, and easily lost the replay.

Back in 1921 Roger Wethered carelessly trod on his ball on the fairway during the Open and had to add the penalty shot. He said it made no difference, because if his round had been a stroke lower he might have played less effectively the next round. In the event he tied and had to be persuaded to turn up for the play-off — he said he'd promised to play in a village cricket match and didn't want to let the chaps down.

Then we had Roberto de Vicenzo signing his Augusta US Masters card for a 4 when millions of TV interviewers had seen him take a 3. If his actual 3 had been allowed, he was into a tie with Bob Goalby. But it wasn't allowed and Roberto, with the 1967 British Open under his belt did not win the Masters this or any other year. But perhaps he profited in the end for that incident gave him a world fame which still continues — but hands up those who've heard of Bob Goalby?

A most interesting incident in Britain was revealed only on film and concerned Bobby Locke, a most meticulous competitor. He won the Open four times and years after the affair on the last green in the 1957 Open at St Andrews he talked about the whole business of putting from the wrong spot, but still collecting the trophy!

Of course it sounds like something from 'Believe-it-or-not'. The blunder was seen later when the triumphant moment was shown on a newsreel film. 'Hold on', said an eagle eye, 'didn't Bobby put a marker into the green wide of the actual spot so his playing partner could putt without interference?' As every golfer knows you mark clear of the other chap's line so your marker doesn't deflect his putt. You do this by lining up on a landmark usually moving your marker a putterhead's distance.

Anyway Bobby had to wait on the last green at St Andrews while his fellow competitor went about his business and all the time the cameras were quietly turning. By the time Bobby came to replace the ball, and putt out for the title, he had forgotten about moving his marker and simply put the ball by his marker, not nearer the hole but also not where his ball had ended after a wonderful approach shot. Not a soul apparently spotted the mistake in the huge crowd. Perhaps they were mesmerised by Locke, who holed out, touched his cap and enjoyed the applause. There were so many things in his mind at that moment after hitting that super second, which had finished some five feet from the flag. 'Even I couldn't believe it', he admitted. His 279 total, in those days, set a new Open record and left Bobby the winner over Peter Thomson by three shots.

Everyone went home happy. They'd seen another fine championship. Then came the film evidence for all to see. The penny dropped. Bobby had not replaced his ball correctly and a famous pro, who shall remain nameless in this book, brought the whole business to the attention of the R and A.

(*left*) Roberto de Vicenzo (*Bert Neale*); (*right*) Bobby Locke en route to an Open win at St Andrews in 1957, his fourth and final win (*Bert Neale*)

Peter Thomson's relaxed address position (*Peter Dazeley Photography*)

Bobby recalls that eight days later they held a meeting. Mr Selway, then on the committee, told Bobby that the meeting had lasted a very long time and in the end they decided to take no action because he'd won by a good margin, had gained no advantage and it was an accident. An interesting problem and those of us who were there know the right man won. A rule was clearly broken but the spirit of the game was observed. Long may this continue.

3
Club Golf

The secretary

Most club golfers in Britain seem to think they could quite easily take on the job of club secretary, should the need ever arise. They rate it an ideal job for those who have retired from the real world. They think that all you need actually do is pop into the golf club at about 10 am, have a coffee brought in by a smiling young member of the staff, browse gently through the post, dictate a few letters, mostly about unpaid subscriptions or querying whether the last delivery of fertiliser really did cost £87 36p and then join the members for a midday session at the 19th hole, to be followed, of course, by a light but nourishing lunch and eighteen holes of golf.

When you consider the turnover of even a quite ordinary golf club, you realise that the job of secretary or manager, the title I would prefer, is a very important one and worthy of full-time training. It would appear that members are rather loathe to pay proper subscriptions to golf clubs and in consequence many golf clubs cannot, therefore, see their way clear to paying a substantial salary to someone to run the club.

Committees, and club members even more so, also seem to think that an annual subscription of £200 is quite horrendous. Well, if you look back twenty years or even less to see what the fees were then, it is, but we are living in an entirely different world. The days of the retired military officer as secretary is certainly past. There are many reasons for this. The Services themselves are changing rapidly. We haven't had a world war, although goodness knows we've had plenty of other types of war, since 1945. And so we are not getting that influx of retired officers looking for that bit of added income and a strong interest in life from the age of fifty onwards.

It would make sense for any club which has, let's say, 600 members, to employ a manager and pay him £10,000 a year and offer him a percentage of the overall profits. If he's in charge of green fees and income from visiting societies, as well as checking on bar staff and the entire greenkeeping team, he is heading a significant group and must surely be worth more than the pittance so often offered these days.

Of course, the club would need their own accountant to keep an eye on where the money has gone and to keep an overall eye on expenditure. And stocktaking, at regular intervals, is obviously required.

A golf club should be run as efficiently as a business. Holiday lists have to be arranged, a wages bill should be typed on one sheet of paper so the efficient, but compact committee, can inspect it at a moment's notice.

Complications arise at many clubs because they charge different rates of subscription. At many, clergymen or Service personnel get in at reduced rates. The elderly, who have been members for many years, are also eligible for special rates; so too are the youngsters. At many clubs women pay considerably less, but mustn't tee off during certain hours and at other clubs there are five-day members who pay less, whilst local police or school children are allowed in to have instruction from the pro under the Golf Foundation scheme, or other cut-price schemes.

Care must be taken with the booking of societies. Clashes must be avoided and great care exercised with competitions, particularly the mid-week ones. Complaints pour into the secretary's office all the time, ranging from the varying price of drinks to alleged rudeness of members and staff and even the suggestion that the professional or his assistant has been making eyes at one of the lady members.

The secretary, therefore, has to be something of a diplomat. But his office can be invaded at almost any hour by a member wishing to pass the time of day, pay his subscription — sometimes on the never-never — or round him up for a game, imagining the secretary can conjure up two more to make the four in a matter of minutes.

When the secretary dares suggest he is a bit too busy to play golf just now, he is branded as being stand-offish and far too big for his boots and he'll never take the place of Fred, who retired two years ago. And all the time there are at least three members who are convinced they could do his job much more effectively, for half the money. And some of them may indeed try to run a vendetta against the secretary until they get him out, and themselves, or someone else, in power.

I have some very clear memories of golf club secretaries. My first was as a young man at Ferndown. There was a splendid gentleman called J. C. Beard who had a very nice house overlooking the then 8th green. It's all been pulled down now and there are blocks of flats there these days. He was a great chap who used to wear check suits and sports jackets and toddled round the course off about twelve handicap. He was very nice, very gentle and not at all fiery — but he commanded respect with his quiet firmness and I have pleasant memories of him as indeed I have of Douglas Bond, retired bank manager and former director of Parkstone golf club. He took on the role of secretary when he retired from the bank. He was, in fact, at the club when they sold it to the members at a very advantageous price of about £18,000 or £20,000, which, for ninety or so acres of prime land, freehold, looking over Poole Harbour was ridiculously cheap.

There were other little parcels of land round the course going ridiculously cheaply. Nobody in the club bought them and the then chairman, Jack Stutt bought them up and built on them and eventually they shot up in value and people complained he had kept it all to himself which was true — but nobody had taken up the for sale offer, or looked ahead.

Anyway back to Mr Bond, who was called 'Daddy' because his dear Norwegian wife, Ena, used to call him that all the time. He was well into his eighties and still going strong. He had the great distinction of having an office extension built specially for him at Parkstone. It was rather like a posh cupboard, the kind you find under the stairs. Of course it's all different now since Gordon Dean, one of those energetic and marvellous captains, managed to influence the club to do some useful alterations during his two-year term of office.

Anyway 'Daddy's' posh broom cupboard was always in apparent chaos but he knew where everything was and every letter that came in simply went on top of the pile and if it was December and someone wanted to know who wrote what five months ago, by some uncanny system he knew where the actual letter lay, within about thirty seconds, and there it was.

Towards the end 'Daddy' did get a little forgetful but there was never any animosity or row within the club. If there were problems or complaints, such as someone being reported for ball searching over the stipulated five minutes, or being driven into, or someone had cut in at the 5th, old Bond had the perfect solution and would say that he quite agreed, and the member was told to put the complaint in writing when he got home and it would go before the committee at the next possible opportunity.

Well, home they went and after a couple of pink gins, an argument with the wife or whatever, they had cooled down and the heat went from them and peace and tranquillity remained at Parkstone. But, sadly, there were certain members not happy with Mr Bond. They wanted him to retire early and were on the look-out for a whizz kid to replace him.

When he finally did retire the club was suddenly faced with appointing a replacement. Lots of applicants rushed forward and finally a new régime took over, some dramatic changes were called for and many began to bob and weave as things were seen to be either black or white. Several secretaries went to the wall or departed and why they left I shall never know because I had long since moved to the wild, rugged beauty of Yorkshire. But whatever it was, it was a long time before the harmonious atmosphere which 'Daddy' Bond had developed returned to Parkstone.

There are huge responsibilities heaped onto the shoulders of most golf club secretaries and Binnie Clark, sadly no longer with us, is remembered for so much work as a secretary, and for his initiative in bringing to professional golf tournaments the splendid Senior Service tournament and the now familiar tented 'village' which began at the Dalmahoy Golf Club in Scotland. Binnie was the promotions manager for Gallahers and it was also Binnie who became involved with Golf Management Services which was started, in fact, by Frank Hunter, a former secretary at Royal Lytham and St Annes, Brigadier C. W. Morton and Lieutenant Derek Holmes. They had all been through the mill and had accumulated all kinds of experience which included chartered accountancy with Hunter, a one-time scratch golfer, well able to provide most of the answers.

Anyway, Clark and Hunter met at the Senior Service tournament in the early 1960s and Hunter created a training course which Clark put into operation. The two men teamed up and, among other things, produced the most excellent *The Duties of a Golf Club Secretary*, directed at a secretary taking up his new position. Frankly, just browsing through it, I found tremendous insights into the big business golf has become, even at small golf clubs. The whole production comes from PO Box 1 Gullane, East Lothian. It starts with an extract which the immortal Bernard Darwin once wrote about golf secretaries.

'Not to make a mystery of our belief,' said Mr Boffin to John Rokesmith, 'we have always believed a secretary to be a piece of furniture, mostly of mahogany, lined with green baize or leather, with a lot of little drawers in it.'

Mr Boffin was right, but he mentioned about the only thing that the secretary of a golf club is not required to do. Holes at which strokes are to be taken against bogey, acid or non-acid theory of greenkeeping, sudden invasions of golfing societies on an outing with provision of caddies and legs of mutton for them, equally sudden invasions of leather-jackets and worms and the leading of punitive expeditions against them, ladies in tears because colonels have driven into them, colonels apoplectic because ladies will not get out of the way — here are just a few of the frightful things which at any moment overwhelm, and I know I could not deal with any one of them.

All these things and many others the secretary has to tackle and even so what he does is not so important as what he is. Above everything else he has to be a man of character who, because he is so, contrives to impress his own qualities and create his own atmosphere in the club. Those qualities and that atmosphere vary, for good secretaries are far from being cast in the same mould, but they have this one thing in common that they make themselves felt. Some of them are obviously full

In the opinion of many judges, Bernard Darwin was the finest golf writer of them all and played in one Walker Cup match as a substitute when he had to report it for *The Times*

of energy and others have a deceiving way with them so that they seem to regard everything with tranquillity bordering on indifference.

It then continues:

Ponder what Mr Darwin had to say because there is wisdom there. Your first day as the new secretary will be strange — you will not know what to do or what you are expected to do. The advice is to start off as you will carry on: do not try to play a part cast for you on the stage, do not try and imitate the man you have succeeded, or anyone else: you must stand or fall on your merits, therefore give them every chance to develop and they will be recognised.

Most clubs in Britain have a president who is a person of some standing in the community. In this country the president seldom has much to do with the general running of the club, and indeed he may not even be a member. No hard and fast rule exists as much depends on the interest he takes or has the free time to take in the affairs of the club. The president is voted to office by the members in general meeting and usually holds office until he relinquishes it. Whether he is a member or not he should receive all notices circulated to members, and he should receive special invitations to important functions.

During his term of office, the captain is the most important member of the club. 'The captain can do no wrong' one hears. He is nominated for office by the past captains, or the general committee, and is elected by the members at the annual general meeting [not always so]. Usually he holds office for one year, and, exceptionally, he may be re-elected for another term. The captain is frequently a businessman who makes time to attend to the affairs of the club and to represent the club at dinners of other clubs and at official functions. He entertains as he considers necessary and often at considerable expense. He receives certain courtesies: his name appears on the honours board, he is entitled to a starting time of his own choosing (in fact he is always given precedence on the tee), he has a reserved parking place, and often has a table reserved in the dining room. A good secretary does all in his power to help the captain in his administration of the affairs of the club.

With many hundreds of clubs throughout the country it is not easy to generalise, but you will find yourself in a club that fits into one of three patterns and managed by two distinct sets of officials:

The land and probably the club house may belong to the proprietor who allows the members the use and enjoyment of the property. The members have wide powers as regards the management of the club, but the proprietor retains control of his property.

A club may purchase the land, and form a company under the Companies Act with a board of directors to administer the property which is rented to the club.

A club which has not formed itself into a limited company normally has trustees and an honorary treasurer in whose names the property and fixed assets are held. These officials are voted to office by the members and remain in office until they resign or die; thus they provide continuity of management.

Officials are common to all three types of clubs and comprise the captain and members of the committee. They are elected by the members in general meeting and hold office for a definite and limited period. They are responsible for running the club with regard to the economy of the clubhouse, the upkeep of the course, the holding of competitions and tournaments, and the granting and revision of handicaps.

The secretary therefore has two sets of principals to serve to be the executive officer of the proprietor or the registered secretary of the limited company or the executive of the trustees. Over and above this the secretary of the club is responsible to the captain, the committee and the members. He must at all times recognise his responsibilities as an officer of the club, and must give all officials proper attention and loyalty. They devote much of their spare time to the running of the club, and they look to the secretary as a full-time employee to produce facts and figures as required.

There are not many proprietors in a position these days to hand over their land for the enjoyment of others, and most clubs are either registered under the Companies Acts, or members' clubs. Golf is big business nowadays, and this is true of individual clubs as well as the major tournaments. The game is now played seven days a week, revenue must be sought after, expenses must be carefully examined. In the face of these facts, the argument is steadily growing that it is not practical politics to ask businessmen to run another business in their spare time. In other words, the running of a club by the captain and committee is becoming outmoded, and one innovation is urgently required, namely the taking-on of a business manager. A business manager is merely another name for a secretary, and the hub of the argument is, whatever title he goes by, he should be capable of running the club efficiently; therefore, to attract men of this calibre salaries must be commensurate. However, old habits die hard and it will be some time before captains and committee are prepared to forego the glamour and prestige of 'running the club'.

The general committee, in some clubs termed 'the council', are elected at the annual general meeting, and usually hold office for three years, retiring in rotation. From this body sub-committees are formed: the finance committee, the house committee, the greens committee. In addition there is usually a handicap and competitions committee, and often a social or entertainments committee. These committees consider the various items under their jurisdiction and make recommendations to the general committee.

The bane of some secretaries is the number of separate committees, the number sitting on each, and the times they consider it necessary to meet. For each an agenda is normally required, supporting information must be ready to hand, with the result that the secretary's presence is called for during the two or three hours the committee is in session; afterwards minutes of what has been decided require to be written. Subsequently the minutes of the various sub-committees are deliberated by the general committee, the recommendations approved, or in some cases remitted back, and these decisions put into effect.

When four or five sub-committees meet regularly every month you can picture the amount of the secretary's time that is involved. All this bears on the new secretary. There is of course the other side of the coin. In some clubs, committee meetings are few and far between. A decision is reached between the captain and the secretary, action is taken, and in due course the fait accompli reported to the members of the committee. In other clubs, the sub-committees meet informally, without agenda or minutes, and the decisions are conveyed to the general committee verbally by the convenor or chairman when anything of importance is incorporated in the minutes.

Secretaries must accept the procedure, at least to begin with! In the fullness of time, officials may be prepared to trust and rely on new judgement about what secretaries do on their own authority.

There is naturally a business atmosphere at committee meetings. Club members are at the club to spend their leisure and they will give the secretary a friendly welcome; however it is as well to remember that every club has its share of difficult members, and tact therefore is a pre-requisite. Some members will pose awkward questions, possibly merely to see how you react, others tend to pontificate; secretaries must learn to cope with all types of queries and shades of opinion.

What would be your snap answer if you were asked 'What is the most important part of a secretary's duty?' Surely to satisfy the members. Secretaries should be pleasant and helpful in their dealings with them for this will react on the rest of the staff who will follow the lead from the top. Fix up a game for anyone without a partner, introduce new members around the club, and generally convey that nothing is too much trouble — particularly when it is! Always be approachable, and it is a good idea to leave the office door off the latch except when engaged; this allows anyone to pop his head round the door informally. It is surprising how gratified members are should the secretary happen to come out of his room and greet them on arrival; not regularly of course but every now and then. One of the difficulties is putting the name to the face, and vice versa. It was an American President who observed that nothing was so sweet to a man's ears as the sound of his own name but this goes sour if you call Mr Brown Mr Jones.

Rules are made to be observed, but in a club rules are there to be quoted to those who deliberately or consistently break them. On the other hand if no one is any the worse off, the Nelson touch does no harm. Members are not schoolboys.

Most clubs have a ladies section with a lady captain, an honorary secretary, and a ladies committee. It is customary for the ladies to run their affairs themselves. Sometimes their subscriptions are collected by the lady secretary although usually this is done along with the men's. The ladies pay their way and bring revenue to the club. They are there to stay, and their numbers are more likely to increase and they will have a bigger say in the running of the club as the years go on.

Secretaries should be punctilious about advising the ladies section of anything approved by the general committee which affects them, for example alterations to local rules, to byelaws, dates when visiting clubs have the courtesy of the tee, and so on. The ladies run their sections well. They are businesslike in the conduct of meetings, they pay subscriptions promptly, and generally give the secretary less trouble than do their husbands! At open tournaments they make themselves useful as markers on the course and as helpers on the catering side. Do not underrate them!

The boys and girls today are the full members of tomorrow, so educate them in the faith. Some clubs run juniors sections with an eye to the future of the club and to foster talent at county and national level. Encourage the children: competitions for them in the holidays promote keenness, and the professional will be only too willing to give them a lesson or two.

Well, as you can see, that working paper is obviously full of good advice. You can see they are subjected to all kinds of pressures, one of which concerns new members. At most clubs there is a waiting list and proposers and seconders often tackle club officials as to why old so-and-so has not been elected yet. It would appear to be much easier if you are twenty-five years of age, of good stock and play to scratch. But the fact that you are a good chap, aged fifty-five and off twelve handicap could mean you wait for ever to get into the local club.

The balance is very difficult. I still believe that most golf clubs, in fact, have fewer members than they can accommodate. People seem to think that 500 members or so means the club is absolutely full but if one could speed up play a little, stagger memberships a bit and persuade members to get used to fitting in times of play, meaning that not every member tries to get off the first tee at 9.30 am or 2 pm. They seldom tee off at 8.30 am or 11.45 am or 3.30 pm or, as they say on the railway, at off-peak times. Most clubs have peak hours, though these will differ a little from club to club. On a Saturday, for instance, this tends to be between 8 am and 9.30 and then again in the early afternoon and on a Sunday there is always a formidable crowd between 8 and 9 am. When the four-balls are completed, there is still time for a few jars before Sunday lunch. Again, there are the early afternoon golfers. During the week in summer, and for the rest of the weekend teeing-off hours, things are usually very quiet indeed except for a rush after the offices and factories have closed. It is the weekdays that could most easily accommodate an increase in membership and I am in favour of clubs considering extending the scheme of five-day memberships which at present tends to be reserved for the retired.

Also helpful is the weekend starting sheet. With this system, the secretary puts up a list of time slots at approximately ten-minute intervals and members book up starting times for their four-balls and gaps can be left through the day for those who do not wish to arrange a game too much in advance. This system ensures that the course is more evenly used during summer weekends and is particularly useful in the winter for players — they know exactly when they are down to play and avoid having to cluster in shivering groups waiting their turn to play at 7.30 am.

If you don't believe all this, then look to see how many holes are empty at the weekends, with most members bunched up and waiting for each other, simply because they all insist on teeing off at traditional times. You may argue that they are concerned about meal times at home, or the bar being closed at certain times in the club, but concessions can be made and, in a crowded Britain, will obviously have to be made in the future.

I've seen this system working well at, for instance, Parkstone, where they have a tremendous through-put of visitors and members and it was a rare thing indeed for a golfer to go home without getting a game because of overcrowding.

Apart from all these duties and dramas, the golf club secretary has to run the annual general meeting, while giving the impression that the captain is actually in charge. The secretary has to sit in on committee meetings, keep proper minutes, brief the captain or the head of one of the sub-committees about any awkward questions that might be asked. But not many actually listen to words spoken at the golf club AGM, unless there is some dreadful scheme proposed. But even then, they don't really listen, but just shout.

The secretary is supposed to steer such meetings and Mr Captain, acting as chairman, must be impartial, well informed on the rules of procedure, good tempered, speak in a pleasant tone and try to move the meeting on in good spirit.

This doesn't always happen as some trouble-maker from the back of the hall will ask why the subscriptions have shot up alarmingly, and why the younger members cannot pay their subscriptions on the never-never, say four times a year, which would add further to the administration time.

The secretary sits beside the captain, ready as ever to hold his hand, provide cold water to drink and advice to heed. But also there should be the club's legal representative, surely, and any other professional skills which may be required if things get difficult. But we don't live in a perfect world and it so often falls to the secretary to act as stand-in if, say, the auditors aren't present.

So you see it isn't easy for a secretary and I haven't even touched on some of the instructions he receives from the ordinary member about a certain other member who has gone into the dining-room in jeans, or plimsolls or without a tie — 'And what on earth are you going to do about it?' — knowing full well the secretary really doesn't want to tangle with that particular youth, whose father happens to be his bank manager, or next year's mayor.

You may think some of these things are exaggerated. Well, maybe. But not too much.

Then the indoor staff may be upset when members demand extra boiling water with their tea for two because they notice it has suddenly turned into tea for four. Why should they pay extra when there are plenty of tea bags in the pot so 'Just bring a couple more cups and we'll be fine.' All that running around and if the steward has dared ask for an extra 10p the wrath of God will be brought upon him!

It is quite extraordinary how people will go to restaurants or hotels and willingly pay fortunes for food, whereas at golf clubs so many expect all the prices to be subsidised or give-away. No wonder secretaries wilt.

Some clubs are now financially sophisticated. Whether inflation makes it that way doesn't matter; the fact is the golf club takings are very substantial, with green fee receipts and society takings perhaps at £50,000 and bar takings, for quite humble clubs, even more than this.

So if you stand back and tot it all up, you find the income of a quite average club is more than £100,000. As a matter of fact a chum has shown me the figures for a club ten miles from London. It has just one pretty course, which runs through silver birch and it earns £145,000 in an average year. It pays out £78,000 on the course, clubhouse and in wages to a good staff, some of whom are part-time and some of whom are earning overtime.

The secretary gets around £6,000 a year; there is a bill for pensions, printing, postage and stationery amounting to almost £3,000; auditor's fees at £800; legal and professional charges in excess of £1,000; contributions to staff pension funds amount to £7,000; staff meals come to more than £5,000 a year — and so on.

How anyone can pretend that administering all this is a pushover I don't begin to understand.

Plenty of attack in this shot from Dai Rees (*Michael Hobbs*)

And yet I must tell you many clubs are being run by part-timers and are sometimes exploited by half the tradespeople in town. 'We're all right here, lads — it's for the golf club. They've tons of money and we can charge top whack.'

So obviously a golf club needs a financial expert to keep affairs in order. And we haven't mentioned the job of keeping handicaps in line with reality. Some clubs allow dear old Smith to stay on five handicap just because he'd be cross to be put on a sensible figure of eight, where he might feel much more comfortable, and start winning the odd 50p piece instead of being the obvious passenger in any four-ball.

Dear Henry Longhurst used to say handicaps didn't much matter as long as everyone related to everyone else and members could stand straight when they told their handicaps. But these days amateurs travel, and you have only to talk to Dai Rees, who goes out to pro-ams in Bermuda and other far-flung places to know that British club golfers, on balance, are not as efficient as the American ones, who come over and shoot the daylights out of Castle Harbour, returning better-ball scores of around 58!

The sooner someone brings in a computerised system of handicapping, the better. I know these things cost money to begin with, but much money can be saved by them. Imagine looking through the cards of, let's say, 200 competitors. The secretary will examine the scores 'Look, there's John Smith off five — he took three 7s and got round in 79 so maybe he can stay on five.'

Then there is someone who took 11 on the last hole and if he hadn't had this collapse he'd have been round in 85, so better pull him, or put him up, or whatever interpretation is placed upon the round. But thinking has to be done. Golf clubs have an obligation to the game, and the hard work falls mostly on the shoulders of the secretary.

Can you wonder why some of them suddenly walk out when they are not given support?

The captain

In many ways, all the club captain normally looks for is a peaceful year. He heads a committee which itself changes every few years. He knows his term of office is so short there is really very little he can achieve, particularly if there is little cash to be spent as well as, possibly, some narrow thinking.

No proper business could possibly run itself with an ever-changing group of directors, yet golf clubs try to soldier on in this way.

Interestingly, I find there is a great deal more pomp and ceremony at clubs in the north of Britain than ones in the south. In the north one continually hears club members greeting their captains thus on a Sunday morning: 'Good morning Mr Captain' and the reply goes: 'Good day to you Lady Captain, how are you?' and we get the refrain: 'I'm fine thank you, Mr Vice-Captain' and so on with a great deal of formal chat which is, in a way, pleasant but it can go on rather a long time, particularly if you've heard it twelve or more times on every visit!

But the captain, you see, regards his appointment to the office as an important landmark in his golfing life and it's right that this should be so. He drives into office, watched and photographed by other members. Sometimes this ceremony is followed by a few holes, usually with former club officers — but always it is concluded with a delightful time at the bar because captains more often than not drive in on the most chilly and miserable days.

At the annual dinner they wear their bold pink jackets proudly, give away the Captain's Prize and make speeches. Many, of course, do a lot more, such as donating a carpet, or chairs. Some hold cocktail parties, possibly to raise funds. Other captains simply push the boat out with a cocktail party as a way of saying thank you to club officials and friends, and because cocktail parties are good, clean fun.

135

How are captains elected? Well, this can be by a variety of methods. Sometimes past officers elect the new captain; sometimes the outgoing captain selects his own successor; sometimes he is chosen by the committee; and sometimes he just evolves, as the leader of the Conservative party used to, with no one — including the new captain himself — being at all sure how the whole thing has come about. However it is done, most club captains are elected because they are either good fellows, or have done a lot of good work within the club already, or perhaps, the cynical may say they have more money than sense and 'We might get something out of them for the club.'

Well, I'm sure that's happened many times and the new captain ends up buying a new flagpole or resurfacing the car park or doing other far-flung and exotic things. This can be deeply frowned on by prospective captains, who may shy away from the job because they feel they cannot afford such wild and generous gestures. They feel their lack of funds will tell against them and this is a sad part of club life because it's too easy, if you've got the money, to walk into the bar and make friends with everyone in sight by pushing the boat out and buying drinks all round.

But it takes a lot of thought, effort and style — plus personality — to make people feel you've done a marvellous job of being captain without breaking your bank balance. Thank goodness there are still captains like that around, ones who temper the money side, with personality. However, the cry still goes up that an overspending captain may be spoiling it for the next chap.

The amount of work a captain does at different golf clubs can vary very widely. At one extreme, being captain means that the club has honoured you and expects little from you except to drive yourself in, be present at the right time to present the trophies and make a bit of a splash on captain's day. At the other extreme, the man's life can be tied to his golf club for most of the year, particularly from April to October. Let's see what this can add up to, during that six- or seven-month peak period.

1   Select the team and be present at all home and away matches (say one evening a week).
2   Attend one full committee meeting a month and a host of other minor ones during the season (say one evening a week).
3   Arrange and attend a varying number of friendly matches against other clubs — the kind in which the higher handicap players can take part (say half a dozen during the season).
4   Attend throughout competitions (say one full day a week).
5   Be at all times ready to jump to it when there is a crisis: the greenkeeper is off indefinitely; the steward has run away with the lady captain; the Toro had broken down; the brewery drivers are on strike; the police have just

been to say that the club have forgotten to renew their licence and the bar must be shut down until one is obtained; the new fertiliser being tried out has scorched all the greens; the secretary has accepted bookings from three visiting parties for the same teeing-off times and they are all now arguing on the 1st tee and the secretary has shot himself. Exaggerated perhaps — but only if the captain has a fairly trouble-free year . . .

One final word about golf club captains. Not long ago I had the pleasure of going to the Stand (Lancashire) golf club which was celebrating its seventy-fifth year. Peter Hopkinson was the captain during 1979–80. A youngish man, enthusiastic and successful, he was an excellent captain in every way although he wasn't to everyone's taste. He took the club by the scruff of the neck and managed to generate money and spent about £30,000 on the course which, as we've said before, is the heart of a club because the course is where the real income is derived from.

Peter Hopkinson may have ruffled a few feathers because he was considered by some to be too wealthy and brash, but he did it all with such flair that the enthusiasm generated at the club was enormous.

Committees

Committees are all too often more hindrance than help, and not just because too many serve on them. They have strange ways of finding members a niche on the various sub-committees. So often the wrong man is put on the wrong sub-committee. I remember when a boy at Ferndown, we had two men on the committee whom I knew well.

One was E. C. M. (Ted) Stewart, whose father had a huge landscape-gardening business in the area. The other was a splendid publican who for many years ran the Bear Cross Hotel on the outskirts of Bournemouth. He was Bob Hill. They both went on the committee and who was asked to serve on the house and wines committee? Well, you've guessed it. Yes, Ted Stewart — and on to the greens committee went Bob Hill.

You wonder how these apparent mix-ups come about. One suspects that someone on committee feared that Bob Hill might have tried to introduce some special lines of wine into the clubhouse and might have been too involved, and after a little profit for himself. And they might have thought Ted Stewart would influence the club to buy a forest of trees. Well, of course, the answer is that if you have that attitude it's sad. Money is wasted at clubs by committees buying the wrong type of tree, quite unsuited to the ground, and they all die, leaving a hole in the finances. Or someone on the wines committee decides there is a tremendous wine offer in some far-off spot and a great purchase is made, only to find it is part of that French fraud and more suited for the head greenkeeper to use to rub down the teak chairs situated near certain tees.

Oh, yes, you see it's difficult. But many clubs run on efficient lines. Take Luffness in Scotland, a place where I've played many times, and always enjoyed. They, apparently, don't believe in over-administration. It has a compact committee, meeting only a few times a year, which eliminates all kinds of discussions at meetings which, at some clubs, go on and on and on — and on! Such meetings last sometimes until deep into the night, spiced with whisky or gin, brought in by a smiling steward who begins to realise, late in the piece, that apart from being way past his bedtime, those in charge are about to make important decisions while having, how shall we say, not the clearest of heads.

Then we get the snooker fans for the committee to deal with. They hate to

A golf clinic is always popular with the members. Here Rees is telling them how to do it and Max Faulkner is about to do it. Seated (left to right) John Jacobs, Bernard Hunt and yours truly seem to have heard it all before

wait and there is a feeling that perhaps the golf club should have two tables because one does hate to wait to play. They must be kept in immaculate condition and I must tell you that I have experienced a system of light meters into which you fed coins and when the time expired, the lights went out! This method did generate quite useful income for the club as it was fail-safe but as the club was old-established, certain folk considered it a bit infra-dig so it went back to the old system of a card on the wall and you write your name down. The charge is 30p an hour and you are on your honour to pay in the special box. It's strange how suddenly the snooker income went from quite a considerable annual sum to just a few pounds.

As I've said in my opinion golf club subscriptions should start at about £250 a year. Now, before you all have the most awful fit, that works out at around £5 a week, quite a bit less than the average green fee if you chose to play 52 times a year. Put another way, it is probably less than smokers spend each years on cigarettes, cigars and matches.

You cannot expect to have really tip-top club facilities unless prepared to create income within the club. I've always felt that subscriptions should pay entirely for the running of the club and any other money coming from what-ever source, including green fees, one-armed bandits, films, raffles and so on, should be put in a fund for club improvements and development.

So the situation inside the clubhouse is a difficult one and can lead to much discussion, and the exchange of opinion as to the exact function of the clubhouse, which started life years ago as just a place in which to change one's shoes in decent privacy.

Stewarding

What of the steward, and wife? They are indeed a breed apart. The difficulty is getting the balance right. Think how many *couples* you actually like. You say to yourself: 'He's nice, but she's a bit tricky' or 'What a super girl she is, but how on earth does she put up with him?'

Look at yourselves. How many times do we men try to keep the peace in order to continue a friendship? It's the same situation for the steward and stewardess. She may be excellent in the kitchen but have no presence in the bar and we all know she loves a drop of mother's ruin, or for those not familiar with that tipple, the High and Dry gin bottle! This means a couple of disasters a month which may take great skill to smooth over.

Then, you may get a highly efficient steward, straight as a die, but some may say his manner behind the bar is rather brusque and he *will* insist on closing bang on time — never popular with golfers. Some critics say he is a bit pushy, and his children make an awful noise. Or that his wretched dog barks. They they add remarks like 'Do you know, this beer seems to be thinner than when we had old Jackson here, our last steward.' Some stewards are indeed accused, and occasionally found to be diluting the mixture.

The perfect steward and stewardess, according to many, should be dressed smartly, but not too stylishly, should whip up a meal of bacon and eggs at first light, served with crusty home-made bread, provide freshly-made coffee, and should produce lunches at £2.75 which must include two kinds of soup, roast beef or Dover sole, fresh vegetables, pie made specially by the stewardess and served with real, yes real, ice cream. This should be followed by the cheese board, celery in season and lashings more coffee with, for the regulars, the occasional peppermint creme thrown in at no extra. Of course any catering person can tell you this simply isn't possible, at the price.

Then you get the weekend card crowd. The steward will be expected to stay up half the night with them, making small talk, and if the lads suddenly feel a bit peckish, well of course the stewardess can be asked to leave the best part of the Parkinson TV show and come way from her first sit-down of the day to cut some sandwiches. And it won't end there. Certainly Mr Smith can have brown bread, with the crusts left on, and Mr Jackson can have his sandwiches with white bread, and the crusts off and Mr Green can most certainly have French bread and cheese.

Someone else may want boiled eggs or nuts to go with his pink gin and all this individual attention must come in a day's work. And if you dare suggest that the subscription should go up, or that overtime payments be offered, then it's nightmare time at the annual general meeting where, I'm given to understand, many words are spoken, but few heeded! Probably just as well.

Sometimes it's not easy for the staff at clubs to totally respect members because they know certain golfers have a habit of removing newspapers, magazines, writing paper and even soap and toilet paper. Many members actually boast that they only come down to the club to have a shower because that saves the heating at home and there are some lovely towels there now, which cuts down on the laundry!

Those, slightly more thoughtful, only remove newspapers that are a day old, or magazines which are not totally topical and, at today's prices, they may have a point. I know of one gentleman who used to claim the expensive magazines he took away were for an old people's home, and they were — his wife was the old person. I also know that some clubs have put out quite expensive men's toiletries in the locker room, only to find them gone in a flash. And then the assistant pro, or the steward, is unfairly accused.

This type of member seldom contributes to the staff Christmas Fund and if he does, puts in only £2, pointing out that the fund is subject to tax anyway. Or that he wasn't happy about there being no tea, one Saturday last winter when, admittedly, the whole place was twelve inches under snow. That sort of member changes in his car, doesn't buy much more than half a bitter in the club and buys his cigarettes down the road, where they are 2p off. Likewise he stocks up from the cut-price off licence in town and will not, under any circumstances, buy his liquor from the golf club, which would help its profits and he is, after all, something of a shareholder. This is the member who protests when the subscription has to go up because the annual turnover is down.

Please don't bombard me with letters saying your club isn't like this because I must confess my observations are made with tongue in cheek, remembering, however, what we have all found in our travels. But unhappily it does have a ring of truth to it.

The professional

My family has been connected with golf since 1919. I suppose with a half smile on the face, you'd say the job is fairly straightforward. Most clubs want their pro to play as well as Neil Coles or Arnold Palmer. They don't mind if he goes away playing in four local tournaments and whenever the twenty-eight-man committee meet and give clearance, he can play up to six tournaments, providing he uses his annual holiday allowance for at least two of them.

The professional is expected to be part psychiatrist, part public relations expert and must have a wife who will take an interest in his job and play the game (but not too well lest the lady members point out she is getting free lessons and free balls). The pro's wife might be allowed to be an honorary member without going on the waiting list, which will be regarded as one of the perks.

His shop must be on a par with a modest Harrods and must offer discounts equal to Aladdin's Cave or Tesco. It must have very generous credit facilities without any thought of interest and offer some of the best trade-in terms for some of the oldest clubs you will ever see. You see, golf clubs made in 1950 which were probably bought for about £1.50 apiece by the mere fact of inflation might well seem to be worth £5 or £6 each, but they are not worth that to the professional.

So one must look at the price of old clubs rather as the dealers look at second-hand cars. And in golf dealings with members, the client will almost certainly want top price for his old clubs, *and* something off the new set for which he's doing a part-exchange deal. When the total settlement comes to,

The number plate is my way of saying 'If you can't beat them, join them'. Sorry about the spelling

say £108 he will suggest, with a flourish, that the figure be rounded down to £100. And he will expect half-a-dozen balls to be thrust into his hand by the ingratiating professional!

As well as all this, the local professional must be a very good after-dinner speaker because he will be expected at the Rotary, the Lions, or the Masonic Lodge. He will have to be well dressed, but not effeminate, yet mustn't upstage the captain. He will have a car but colour schemes here are important and flashy yellow foreign cars with words on the side of them, like 'Le Car', are discouraged.

The pro must be instantly available to play with anyone at a moment's notice and must be prepared to give group tuition to either the ladies or the youngsters at very little cost, which will come under the ever-growing heading of 'putting something back'.

There are other things the pro must not be found doing, like playing thirty miles from home with one of the lady members, even if it is in the mixed alliance meeting, or whatever. This is liable to lead to some heavy gossip. The pro, you see, must handle all members with kid gloves because all of them regard him as a cross between a friend and an employee. This can be awkward when two members have fallen out and one of them is in the shop talking to the pro, when the undesirable chap is seen heading that way. First member shoots out of the shop with a remark about how he can't stand old so and so — 'Isn't he dreadful?' Then the other chap enters the shop and says 'Oh, I see that rotten chap has been in here, I can't stand him. What do you think of him?' If the pro says he agrees, he is in a nasty spot because the next day the two members might have made it up and be drinking whisky together, and swearing eternal friendship. And if one discovers the other has been talked about in a bad light by the local pro then things can be very awkward indeed.

So, you see, it's not easy. And yet there are members who think the pro has a simple life, in a rent-free shop selling to a captive audience. What they forget are the long hours, from daylight until dusk.

My father, from April until October, never worked less than a 90-hour week and many northern pros find they have to make a living in the evening when the offices have shut and the golfers stream out for golf. They work well over a hundred hours a week which, I think, compared to the 35 to 40 hours a week some of our 'brothers' complain about, is rather a joke

My father (left) in 1949. Hands in pockets is Patrick Campbell, undoubtedly the funniest golf writer of them all (or do I hear you say 'What about P. G. Wodehouse?'), next to him Laurie Ayton and then Dai Rees (*Sport & General*)

although I will admit I'd rather be in a golfing surrounding than in a factory.

Greenkeepers

So far I have been discussing mainly what goes on inside the clubhouse so let's now step outside on to the course. After all it's what a golf club is really all about. If the snooker room is a joy, the lounge bar elegant and the locker room inches deep in rich carpeting, all will still be lost if the tees are bare, the fairways weedy and the greens not true. All too often we find that clubs really ought to spend more money on the course, giving the greenkeepers a decent salary, the best tools to do the job and good working conditions. Too often you still see old army-type vehicles, kept in service because the club refuses to buy the latest equipment. In the USA they spend lavishly on both course and clubhouse; here we tend to concentrate on new curtains for the ladies, good beer and a new cloth for the snooker table. No club puts every spare penny into the course.

If a club has a good greenkeeper, or the son of a greenkeeper who has been there for years and years, he deserves support. He doesn't need a selection of unqualified greens committee types telling him where he's going wrong. This is where certain committee men can be dangerous because, as we all know, 'a little knowledge . . .'

If the course is in good shape it should be left to those who understand. Though beware the dreaded agronomist, an 'overseer of land', or 'husbandry of land', as one dictionary puts it. There are several of them about. Like other 'professional' men they seem to disagree with each other's analyses. Some believe courses are over-watered and/or over-fertilised, while others say anything other than organic matter is to be avoided at all costs.

It's up to your greenkeeper to decide but make sure that the advice he is getting is at least professional and does not come from the chairman of the greens committee alone. Invariably he is an amateur but all too often does not behave as such. And worse, at too many clubs half the membership regard themselves as both knowledgeable about the green-keeping art and no mean golf architects either. They pester their greenkeeper with advice and criticism that is always contradictory.

Now don't run away with the idea that I'm bitter. This has been a professional golfer's observation of life within a golf club over thirty-five years and a family history going back sixty years in the game.

I feel that some administrations are too top heavy with well-meaning folk who, if asked to design a horse, might come up with a camel. If there is a moral in all this, it is that if you have a good greenkeeper, for goodness sake leave him alone, encourage him and if he is not well paid, then who can you blame if he departs elsewhere to a more enterprising establishment just down the road?

If we are serious about raising our standards we must seek information from America and Canada where worse climatic conditions of heat and cold are endured successfully. After a hard winter, Canadian greens recover in a couple of months while it can be two years here. Again, there is much theory and little sense about the use of water. 'Don't do it', they say, 'make the roots grow down.' Better to find out when and how much your own greens should be watered than this archaic dictum. All in all, too much is done without clear evidence being obtained that it is the right thing to do.

Joining a club

At many clubs anyone wishing to join must know several existing members who can write in to the club on his behalf saying that he is an ideal chap to become a member. This, of course, is not always possible. Also I feel sorry for children, or youngsters, who have been introduced to the game by the Golf Foundation: their parents perhaps don't play and obviously they want

Hot work in the Bahamas for Arnold Palmer

to join a golf club in order to continue a sport they were briefly shown while at school.

I get about thirty letters a year, from non-playing parents, who ask what their offspring should do in order to get into a club. All I can recommend is that they go along to the club, have a word with the secretary, and state their position. Youngsters need encouragement and some clubs are first-class in this respect, and certain members devote a lot of time to the young while golf professionals often give them a leg up in the sport, remembering what it was like for them in years gone by. Even a Palmer or Ballesteros were faced by difficulties in plenty.

In the old days it was enough to have a proposer and seconder, but not always so these days. At some clubs a prospective member will require sixteen signatures or letters from people who recommend him to the club and even then the newcomer may have his name posted on a board. And one blackball in committee can then keep someone out of the club, and into oblivion. And yet a committee member is not obliged to give a reason why he blackballed someone; it may result from a personal vendetta going back years.

Rightly or wrongly, golf clubs do not have to give an explanation for rejecting a golfer as a member. Some say certain clubs do not have members of a particular religion, whether they be Catholic, Jewish or Protestant. I remember a friend of mine reporting his interview for membership at one London club. He was asked four questions: 'What does your father do?', 'What do you do?', 'How much do you earn?' Then came what might have been the most important question for that committee: Are you Jewish? The friend replied to the first three questions. To the last he replied: 'Mr Chairman, I no longer wish to be considered for membership.' Thank goodness the Jewish clubs don't take that attitude and ban Gentiles from their excellent courses.

Some other clubs say they don't have any tradespeople although whatever that means these days I really don't know. Do they mean they exclusively cater for the professions? If they do, members must be pretty thin on the ground.

4
The Ladies

We live in a world of change and nowhere is this more noticeable than in women's golf. Some of the changes have been for the good, some unexpected. What intrigues me is that at certain clubs there has been no change at all. In a time of liberation for women, we still find unbending males resisting the winds of change.

I know there are ladies clubs where men are allowed — under supervision! — so we must move cautiously into this debate. But let me right away declare an interest. I have always been a supporter of women's golf because I believe they keep most clubs going — from Monday to Friday.

And I can understand their fury at being told they must use a side door, or avoid being seen near the men's bar window, or not able to tee off during certain hours, or sit on the verandah. Frankly, it is all rather strange but I cannot totally condemn the fortresses of men-only golf because they, too, have tremendous appeal. The difficulty of mixed golf is co-existence and one finds cranky golfers of both sexes who cause havoc.

What surprises me is the length of time ladies golf has been around in Britain. Just look at the *Golfer's Handbook* and you'll find that in 1893 we had the ladies' championship, two years before the men's amateur championship, which shows how the girls clearly demonstrated their initiative. The original lady winner was Lady Margaret Scott who won it three times in a row.

It's true the men had started the Open championship belt in 1860 but only eight competitors turned out at Prestwick where Willie Park won. In those days a woman who wished to swing a golf club across her chest must have been regarded as a strange animal indeed, and one has to admire the way they gradually overcame our restrictive ideas about women in sport.

Just look at the famous names who took part in golf and added lustre to a game which is perfect for women. Cecil Leitch and Miss Hezlet were the most significant before the Great War. Then we had more champions, the

(*left*) The runner-up, Cecil Leitch, and the winner, Joyce Wethered, just before the final of the 1920 British Ladies Amateur Championship; (*right*) Joyce Wethered in the 1930s

most famous being Joyce Wethered who was tall, elegant and a beautiful swinger of a golf club.

And there was Doris Chambers who also won the ladies title and Diana Fishwick who later married Brigadier Critchley and, of course, Enid Wilson who won three English championships in a row and loved the game so much she took to writing about it on *The Daily Telegraph* and always kept cheerful despite the raised eyebrows and remarks about amateur status.

Then came Pam Barton, a most attractive woman sadly killed during World War II, Wanda Morgan, Jessie Anderson, Jean Donald and after the war the delightful Frances Stephens, and the Vicomtesse de St Sauveur, a beautiful winner in 1950. There was Philomena Garvey, a tough competitor from Ireland, Elizabeth Price of the slow, easy swing, Marley Spearman, who brought her training and discipline as a dancer to bear on the game, Brigitte Varangot and Catherine Lacoste from the Continent and so many other names we in Europe will always remember.

Just look through the record book and discover the girls' championship winners. Famous names like Angela Ward, who married another winner

Michael Bonallack, Ruth Porter, who won despite her tiny size, and fair-haired Diane Robb and the youngest-ever winner Nancy Jupp, who now helps organise the US *men's* Open!

In more recent years we have enjoyed watching Dinah Oxley and Pam Tredinnick and the overall standard of play has become better and better with good competitors adding to the quality of a championship which started way back in 1919.

Then the Welsh girls', the English girls', the Irish and Scottish girls' championships began and all produced grand winners who played so well that many quite good men performers were almost too scared to play against them, and when they did they found the weaker sex quite content to play from the men's tees — thank you very much.

And all the time the ladies were running their affairs under the guidance of the Ladies Golf Union. It may not have always been perfect, but I'm now coming round to the view that they got it right. If, for instance, the ladies don't play enough competitive golf then, sorry, but up goes the handicap which leads to anger from the girls because only the wicked cheat really wants a high handicap, most of us having a delightful vanity about ourselves which means that handicaps, both of men and women, tend, if anything, to be too flattering.

(*left*) Sally Bonallack and her mother, formerly Angela Ward (*Sidney Harris*); (*right*) Sally Little, as pretty as any on the US circuit (*Peter Dazeley Photography*)

Top tournament pro Judy Rankin is almost frail looking but with her basically shut-face method she hits a low, rolling ball a good distance. She shows about four knuckles of the left hand (*Peter Dazeley Photography*)

The point I have been trying to get across is that ladies golf is massive, it's been with us for donkeys years and why some men still allow themselves to get hot under the collar if they so much as see a woman on the course is beyond me.

American professional women's golf really took off after World War II but other countries, Australia, and most of the European countries all viewed the paid lady players with doubt — for a while.

The United States ladies events didn't begin until 1930 when some startling players like Glenna Collett set the ball rolling. One ought to remember, too, that our girl Pam Barton won both the US and British titles and set an example all over the world and showed ladies could play a sport, and still remain attractive and feminine.

The US amateur went to Laura Baugh in 1971 and later she turned professional and strode the fairways like a jewel, but did not win. However, just watching her play was enough for many spectators.

The way for Miss Baugh had been paved by some remarkable lady players who paid entrance fees to tournaments and hit the golf ball for money, starting in 1946 when Patty Berg cleaned up. It was in 1948 that probably the most outstanding woman golfer of all time hit the headlines. Babe Zaharias struck the ball more powerfully than most men. She was so good that she beat top men amateurs of her day, and from the same tees. One of her victims was Leonard Crawley, golf writer and sportsman extraordinary. He tried to show her to the ladies tee for their Men *v* Women clash. The famous Babe said: 'No thanks, Len, the back marker will do me fine!' and she won, easily, playing level.

Women's golf had seen nothing like her until one day she fell ill and died from cancer. But women's golf went ahead and we saw other big hitters like Joanne Gunderson, Anne Quast, Mickey Wright, Betsy Rawls and the Canadian Marlene Stewart, who proved so popular here in Britain.

Certain ladies dominated for a few years: Donna Caponi Young, Carol Mann, Judy Rankin, Nancy Lopez and there grew up a US women's circuit which offered more money than the European men's tour and brought lady golf stars to the US TV screens in competition, and in commercials recommending washing-up liquid and the rest.

And in Britain we were delighted with the women's pro circuit. Michelle Walker from Kent turned professional under manager Mark McCormack.

Michelle Walker. Contrast the clubhead aim at the top of the swing with Judy Rankin's (*Peter Dazeley Photography*)

She signed in a sunny London garden and was on her way. Others followed, cautiously at first — then a flood. There are now about 35 playing the British circuit and the same number again are still needed.

The British women's tour has a first-class man in Barry Edwards and his wife Carole and from humble beginnings they have made a marvellous start.

The whole business of women's golf has been subjected to much rubbish, talked and written by those who suggest the girls have to be rather masculine to survive a tour that requires life from a suitcase. Perhaps the critics should get out on the course a bit and see just how good girls are at the game. Frankly I think men can learn more from watching the top lady players than they can from watching players such as Palmer, Watson, Nicklaus, Ballesteros et al. These are superbly naturally gifted athletes with a particular talent for accelerating a clubhead to a very high speed indeed. The desk-bound executive is totally incapable of emulating them but he might be able to learn from the measured rhythm of a Nancy Lopez, remembering that she generates enough clubhead speed to move the ball a very respectable distance, further than most men in the higher handicap divisions can manage.

Although the girls are fierce competitors, I find them fun to watch and they don't appear to have been ruined yet. They are not too tense, and find time to talk with their partners in the pro-ams. They are an object lesson in the art of public relations. Long may it be so.

I am proud to be the President of the British Women's Professional Golfers' Association and from that position I know how seldom it is that we hear of bad behaviour among the girls, or about heavy fines being inflicted on them for breach of rules, erratic behaviour — or plain cheating.

Years ago the cruel men said women only took up golf because they were too ugly to do anything else; they weren't able to ice skate or cut a pretty ballroom figure because they had big feet. Men were really opposed to the girls playing 'their' game and intruding into clubhouses built for men only. Even today quite famous clubs will not allow women in, because, they say, there are no ladies facilities.

You may say big business moved into women's golf because it was ripe for exploitation, or because women did the shopping and tend to spend our money for us, so it made sense for the commercial giants to woo them as Colgate did. Certainly in America the promotion of women golfers reached dizzy heights.

There are, however, occasions when the men want to talk together, free of feminine company, including their wives. I suspect that a majority of club members regret the invariable fact that most of the lady members of any club are married to a male member and would welcome a greater leavening

Leading US money winner in 1979 and well up again in 1980: Nancy Lopez Melton (*Peter Dazeley Photography*)

of unattached young beauties to decorate the lounge bar. Though, alas, I always remember the golf writer who used to complain that the girls at his golf club enjoyed drinking gin and tonic like mad, but did not enjoy buying the stuff like mad.

The equal rights campaign enjoyed wide coverage in the newspapers some years ago and however you argue the case, women are not equal in many ways, one of them being in strength. Some lady players on the pro tour in America tried to pack too much golf into their year because the lure of the dollar is great, but gradually they are learning to pace themselves as women, and have stopped trying to prove themselves the equal of men. It is a pointless exercise, really, because we can all enjoy girls' golf, and are doing so.

Is it a very different game for girls, when it comes to the question of instruction?

Sometimes girls ask me just how they can improve, and add to power that obviously they don't have. It's hard to advise an attractive girl to start

Chako Higuchi has got her body well out of the way and her arms can now swing freely through (*Peter Dazeley Photography*)

squeezing springs, or do the occasional press-up or go running. But in some cases this is exactly what is needed. The ladies do tend to loosen their grip during the swing, and very often with an over-long swing this proves fatal to the shot. At the top, the hands don't hang on and the club drops back; on the way back again the hands tighten and regrip with the inevitable result that the swing path goes out of true.

Dai Rees often advises ladies with small hands to try the two-handed baseball grip, which means all fingers on the shaft. This is well worth a try but remember the hands must work together, so don't allow this ten finger grip to let the hands work separately.

A shorter swing with a solid grip can work wonders for both sexes and I've read advice that the ladies should use a low compression ball which gives the clubface more chance to crush the elastic — but I've never felt convinced of this idea! Sensible tips concern the advice to use the lofted woods more frequently if you are not powerful and be worried not at all when a rival uses iron off the tea. Play it your way is the best advice.

One aspect about women which puzzles me — oh yes, there are several — is the way they putt. I feel women should be as good as the men at putting and there is no reason why they shouldn't be better. But my feeling is the boys would outputt the girls in a competition. It's puzzling why some promoter in America hasn't already staged a men *v* women putting contest — maybe they have?

156

My advice for the ladies is not to overswing, sweep the ball away rather than try to thump it.

In my travels I've heard some shocking tales about the way women are treated in golf and most of us can remember the time golfer and journalist Liz Kahn walked boldly into the men-only clubhouse at St Andrews and looked things over in the reading room. Very slowly one old member lowered his *Times* newspaper and looked at the invader. 'Do you know women are not allowed in here?' he asked quietly. Evidently golf-writer Liz tried to explain that she merely wanted to look the place over as part of her job but the old boy lowered his eyes and muttered 'I don't see you.' She was ordered out into the street, pretty quick.

At other clubs women are excluded from the men's bars and the right of men to drink without intrusion is defended in extraordinary ways. An idea went in one club suggestion book that the ladies section 'be removed to the greenkeepers sheds' but this was turned down, the joke went, by six votes to seven from the committee, all-male of course! However, I really do see signs that this sex battle is dwindling.

Looking back into history in this connection is laughable. Women were thought to be of the wrong design for the game and even today, at Royal St George's, Sandwich, they are not recognised and members can drive through them if any actually hold up play on these historic links. They are literally ghosts on the course, and aren't charged a green fee because they do not come into the scheme of things at all! I wonder if this is true or just another golfing tale?

Still men only — the Royal and Ancient clubhouse at St Andrews (*Peter Dazeley Photography*)

5
Course Memories

Over the years golf has been very kind to me, allowing me to travel the world to enjoy the delights and frustrations of a superb pastime. I suppose I could fill half-a-dozen books on my travels and the people I've met over the years but in this chapter I shall concentrate on Britain, with the occasional excursion into Europe.

It's been my great good fortune to play on many fine tests of golf, although strange to say the actual number might not be as high as you might think. I have not, like certain 'collectors' of golf courses — often American — played courses in their hundreds and even thousands or built up a collection of cards and memorabilia from my golfing wanderings.

If I had had a great amateur career before moving into the professional ranks, golfing horizons might have been even more far-flung, and there would, perhaps, have been the glitter of much silver acquired by the winning of trophies. I've never seen anything so impressive as the valuable metal amassed by the great Irish amateur Joe Carr and Englishman Michael Bonallack — talk about the silver vaults! Nevertheless, there are a few about the house and I specially treasure my collection of silver tankards that derive from many years of competing in the Dunlop Masters. Yet as a rule we professionals do not acquire trophies in quantity. True, a cup or the like is presented at the end of most tournaments and championships but, alas, back it has to go a year later.

Instead, we have to be content with pieces of paper with rows of figures on them but useful all the same for settling the bills.

Anyway, although I passed through my amateur days without actually collecting much in the way of trophies, I still played on a choice selection of courses, because of my connection with the Lord Robert's Workshops and the Forces Help Society. We played charity matches as professionals in some wonderful parts of the country. Tournament golf however, is played on much the same circuit year after year and the reasons the courses are chosen are often not strictly golfing ones. There are several other factors to be taken into account. Most of these relate to the need to have spectators and the needs of those spectators. In the first place, the organisers have to go for an area in which sufficient people live to give the prospect of large crowds. (Of course, I'm talking of run-of-the-mill tournaments. You could stage the Open on a raft in the Irish Sea and they'd still manage to turn up!) Once the crowds are assembled there must be ample car-parking space and the course itself should have good vantage points and there must be enough space to allow spectators to move about reasonably freely, room for the erection of stands and a tented village. And at the end of the day, the crowds must be housed and fed.

Britain has the wondrous gift of some of the finest courses in the world. As regards links courses we are particulary blessed. While the USA, for instance, has very few true links courses we have several areas where course follows course in almost unending sequence. Think of the Lancashire coast, the west coast of Scotland from Turnberry northwards, east Kent and East Lothian to both east and west of Gullane Hill. Unhappily some of them are not properly looked after, and many are cruelly overplayed with some famous courses exposed to every rabbit tourist and traveller. At the end of the holiday season I've seen a course such as the West at North Berwick

The 10th tee at Turnberry (*Peter Dazeley Photography*)

(*left*) Tom Weiskopf (*Bert Neale*); (*right*) Tony Jacklin in his great days — taken in 1971. Everything seems to be flowing through the ball (*Peter Dazeley Photography*)

almost unplayable after thousands upon thousands of divots have been chopped from the fairways. In contrast, just a few miles down the road, Muirfield is rigorously guarded by Captain Hanmer. The club golfer must persuade his secretary to write glowingly on his behalf and he may then be allowed to enter the domain of the Honourable Company of Edinburgh Golfers. His efforts will be rewarded with a course in pristine condition and, on a weekday morning or afternoon, hardly another soul to be seen. For the professional who has just finished high up or even won an Open caution is also wise. Ben Crenshaw, perhaps the most intensely interested in golf history of modern players, challenged the 1980 champion, Tom Watson, late in the evening of the final day, to a couple of holes at Muirfield. The crowds departed, they played the 10th and 18th holes with hickory shafts, the occasion enlivened by a bagpiper rendering 'Amazing Grace' and 'Scotland the Brave'. Others, Tom Weiskopf, Tony Jacklin and Tom Kite among them, gathered on the last green to watch their endeavours — and were swiftly dispatched by Captain Hanmer with threats that they might never be allowed to return to the sacred turf of Muirfield.

Lack of money is often the cause of neglect and willing greenkeepers are frequently fighting a losing battle with out-dated equipment. Sometimes, as well, greens committees, lacking in knowledge, plunge blindly into courses and decide to alter holes with no regard, or respect, for tradition.

On the other side of the coin, quite ordinary holes are left unaltered. Bunkers placed to catch a drive hit with hickory remain, or ones placed well short of a green to catch a weak third shot instead punish a well-struck second. Holes originally designed to demand a good drive and a long iron in are today easily plundered by a drive and short pitch. Today, with so many club golfers able to hit the ball very respectable distances, certain courses have failed to move with the times, and fall out of fashion with the good golfer.

In other words, golf in Britain is uneven in quality and the root cause, I suspect, is that we have been getting our sport on a shoestring for too long. We have learned to accept second best, with clubhouses in need of paint and cleaning, insufficient staff and the whole enterprise run by part-timers who mean well but whose main task in life is to earn a living, bring up a family and cope with life outside golf.

However I've been round the world playing golf and know that sometimes when you step onto the first tee at courses in Great Britain, no apologies are needed to anyone — what we have can be superb. Obviously I have my favourites, often because they hosted tournaments in which I played and yes, just now and then, with a trophy and a cheque to follow, probably meaning I've seen the whole thing through rose-coloured spectacles.

Ferndown

My father was appointed professional at Ferndown in Dorset in 1938 and it is here that I'd like to start. We moved into a house just a short walk from the clubhouse, but the clouds of war were gathering and the future was anything but clear. It was not long before father left to join the Dorset Regiment. As he was forty-two years of age, it was rather a rash even if patriotic thing to do. But off he went.

Ferndown was my training ground where I spent my formative years amidst war austerity. It was considered a sort of poor man's Muirfield, very much the gentleman's club. Professionals weren't allowed in the clubhouse, but they built a new pro shop for my father. The old wooden clubhouse had burned down in the early 1930s, so they built a red-bricked clubhouse which faces the wrong way. It would be better swivelled round to look down the course. Now it overlooks the putting green and in the distance there is the 10th tee. The best views are from father's old shop, where Doug Sewell now rules.

I have happy memories of Ferndown. The clubhouse sits on top of a biggish hill which has in view the 18th green and the 1st tee and 6th green, 10th tee and, in the old days, the 9th green was also close to hand. It is a very compact course and was great fun for me as a kid because you could play umpteen series of holes or loops and it was always in beautiful condition, with everything neat and tidy — one reason for so many visitors coming.

I was a good scratch player when I was fifteen and played in the local alliances there, as a boy growing up, and there was a feast of fine courses in the area.

For me the most interesting holes on the old course are the 3rd, a slightly uphill dogleg left to right par 4, the 13th which was laid out by my father and the 16th, named after Harold Hilton. All the short holes are excellent.

Broadstone (Dorset Golf Club)

One of the hardest pars in the country, it can be made a 68 by putting the tee markers back at the 1st hole and a 68 round there is really high-calibre golf. If you scored that with your handicap deducted, you might talk about it for weeks. Perhaps the most memorable hole for me is the short 7th, very long though and difficult with the wind in one's face.

It is crossed by two railway tracks and I can still recall that feeling of excitement when crossing them with another section of the course to follow. The course is wide open with heather, pine and silver birch and its par 3s stand comparison with anywhere in the UK.

Parkstone

In 1957, I had my first full pro job with brother Alec, who now lives in Guernsey. We moved to Parkstone, where Reg Whitcombe, the man who won the windswept 1938 Open, had been for donkey's years. Those days were some of the happiest of my life because, although it was of small acreage, the members made up a good cross section of people, ranging from the wealthy to those who struggled along, and the feeling of camaraderie was considerable.

Parkstone was, in those days, not such a 'tidy' golf club as Ferndown because the ground was a little gravelly and it looked unkempt in places. There were marvellous views across Poole Harbour and Lilliput — yes, that's where Dean Swift wrote Gulliver's Travels — just down at the bottom of the course. Lilliput Road runs through the middle of the picturesque layout.

The finish of the Alliss swing more than 20 years ago when I was at Parkstone; here I am playing at Llandudno in North Wales where I won the PGA Championship in 1957 (*Bert Neale*)

I never tired of playing at Parkstone, in part because of the attraction of heather, pine and silver birch. There are also two lakes which always seemed a particularly brilliant blue, whatever the weather. The 5th is a key hole here, though a relatively short par 4. There is a road and trees on the left and the green nestles into trees with one of the lakes close by. The course, some would say is a little unbalanced for there are five par 3s and five par 5s.

Trevose

But Trevose, on the coast of Cornwall, comes to mind at once. Run by Peter Gammon, it's a cross between inland and links. There are some marvellous holes running along the side of the water and then you come inland for more fine holes, not unlike Killarney in Eire, where you have holes by the famous lake; then inland ones in the second nine.

Trevose is always a delight: grand accommodation, good food and bar, pleasant course — plus a pitch-and-putt layout as well.

Stoneham

Other happy memories for me in the Bournemouth area come from days spent playing in the Strong's tournament. Strong's was a brewery company

I won 20 major tournaments and here is Lord Brabazon of Tara handing over a trophy in 1962 (*Bert Neale*)

based at Romsey that staged a local event in which professionals from the counties which sold Strong's beer would compete. It was taken around to several clubs but, more often than not, it was played at the Stoneham club, that very pleasant, elegant club on the north side of Southampton.

One of my lasting memories of Stoneham is the long, uphill last hole of about 480 yards with that hogsback fairway, bushes and trees either side and that narrow, well-bunkered entrance to the green. How well I remember whizzing a second shot up there to win with a 4. Did I really win that tournament four times? Ah, happy memories. It has a nice old clubhouse with a wooden interior, masses of honours boards and those great dark-green leather chairs which are in the best British clubhouse tradition. It is not on the tournament rota because of the lack of off-course facilities.

Wentworth

For me, favourite golf courses tend to be places where I've done well in tournaments, or had a pleasant exhibition match or day out. Wentworth immediately comes to mind. It was there I won the 1955 Dunlop Professional Tournament over ninety holes and tied for the Daks event in 1963. I also helped win the Wentworth Foursomes with Harold Ridgley, the American master sergeant who reached the final of the Amateur Championship in 1957.

Wentworth was the first really opulent golf club I had ever seen. Detractors say that over the years it has lost its soul and is just a glorified municipal. I think that totally unfair. The clubhouse is huge, the dining-room large and there is a ballroom. The pro shop is a bit far from the centre of things. But the place has that certain magic, probably because I know it so well and over the years I've been able to visit it so many times, working for BBC television, and watching the fortunes of the World Match-Play Championship, first sponsored by Piccadilly Cigarettes and continued so successfully by Colgate and later Suntory.

I remember the professionals there. Jimmy Adams was once pro and Archie Compston played a great challenge match against Abe Mitchell, part of which was at Wentworth. Tommy Haliburton was later professional there, and when he died, his shop passed into the very capable hands of young Bernard Gallacher, another Scot who carries on the fine traditions.

Some of us recall Peter Mills, the Ryder Cup player who, incidentally, has just got his amateur status back again. He was in our winning team in 1957, beating the American captain Jackie Burke at Lindrick emphatically. His mother and father were steward and stewardess at Wentworth for many years and two of his sisters live in Jersey, where Peter Mills now lives as a

successful wine importer, and also runs a flourishing wine bar.

Though now I love the place, as a tournament pro I feared it. There is not an easy hole on the course. If there's a left-to-right wind the drive from the 4th tee is one of the most testing in golf and the finish is as feared as any in golf. From the 15th till one retires gratefully to the clubhouse, the trees seem to march ever inwards.

Sunningdale

Just as Wentworth is full of happy memories, so just down the road is Sunningdale, one of the most famous names in the world of golf. It was here that I won the Sunningdale Foursomes twice, partnered by Jean Donald. What happy days they were, spent on lovely courses, full of pine and

(*far left*) Arnold Palmer approaches the 4th at Wentworth (*Peter Dazeley Photography*)

(*above centre*) Tom Haliburton drives from the 3rd tee at Wentworth in the Dunlop 2,000 Guineas in 1949. Charles Whitcombe is his playing partner (*Sport & General*)

(*below centre*) 'Wild Bill' Melhorn and Bobby Jones in 1926. After that perfect 66 at Sunningdale in an area qualifier for the 1926 Open, Jones went to Royal Lytham and St Anne's and won. Indeed, except for his first attempt, Jones won the British Open every time he entered and in that era, if Jones stayed at home in Atlanta, Hagen took first place

(*right*) John Jacobs in the 1962 Daks tournament at Wentworth (*Sport & General*)

(*above*) Clubhouse and 18th green at Sunningdale (*Peter Dazeley Photography*); (*left*) Clive Clark in 1966 (*Sport & General*)

heather and character and a clubhouse of both elegance and charm, the epitome of what things should be.

Sometimes I wish they had planted a few more trees on the New Course at Sunningdale. Somehow this one is a bit neglected because everyone wants to play on the Old Course, as indeed they do at St Andrews. They want to play the Old at Sunningdale where the immortal Bobby Jones did that perfect round of 66, when qualifying for the 1926 Open.

The Sunningdale characters have been written about by many sports writers. Years ago Open champion of 1904 Jack White was the pro there and later Bernard Drew was secretary. Professional Arthur Lees, whose tales of play are legend, and the caddie master James Sheridan, whose portrait hangs in the clubhouse, became renowned figures and Sheridan wrote a book about his days there.

Sunningdale has a marvellous, relaxed air which typifies what a golf course and clubhouse should be like.

Interestingly my father was offered the pro's job there shortly after the war. He was over fifty, thought himself a bit old and as we were well settled at Ferndown he said 'no'. So Arthur Lees moved from Dore and Totley, in Sheffield, and took over.

I have some marvellous friends at Sunningdale, such as Gerald Micklem who, in his early days, showed such a huge interest in amateur golf and put a great deal into it. Now, in the autumn of his days, he is taking an equal interest in professional golf, quite excellent to see because his sharp brain can be utilised in so many valuable ways.

David Wickens, of British Car Auctions, who has supported British sport so strongly is also a particular friend and knowing such as these makes any return to Sunningdale very pleasurable. Clive Clark, my colleague on the BBC, is now the pro and has a superb shop there.

The Berkshire

Just down the road is The Berkshire, with its two gorgeous courses running through pine and heather. Keith MacDonald has a new and excellent shop there and a day out at the Berkshire is one of the joys of golf. The clubhouse is excellent and the Avia event for ladies comes annually.

Prince's

Moving south-east we come to that marvellous necklace of links on the Kent coast. Prince's is the one I know best and it's a happy stamping ground because I won two tournaments there over the years. One was the PGA

Dave Thomas, with whom I am now partnered in our golf course construction business (*Bert Neale*)

Championship, when I was very nearly laid on the floor to rest, suffering from tonsilitis! I remember it so clearly. I was staying at the Bell Hotel at Sandwich, sharing a room with Dave Thomas and it overlooked the famous waterway and toll gate over the river which added charm, even though some golfers cursed it if they feared a delayed arrival at the bridge while tickets were sold and the border-like formalities dispensed with.

The Bell Hotel had creaking floors, chintz curtains, good solid food and is still a delightful place to stay. Well, the old doctor came in to see his golfing patient and doped me with potions and lotions and I didn't know whether I was going to get through it all, or not. I felt awful and it may have been a good thing because I had no time to think about my putting. I just took it shot by shot, as it came, staggering along and unable to offer conversation to anyone. I went from strength to strength and eventually won, looking like death.

I must confess to wondering whether I had found the golf secret: get a tonsilitis serum and give myself a shot of it; or instead of a 'gee-up' buy some 'drag-me-down' drug to make me quite oblivious to the surroundings. Eventually I decided against it.

Then, in 1969, came the last big event I won. It was the Piccadilly Medal, in those days a match-play knock-out by stroke-play in which I beat George Will in the final at the 37th hole after defeating the reigning Open champion, Tony Jacklin, in the semi-final. I still feel this was one of the pinnacles of my golfing career.

Prince's, I've always thought, is a course with enormous potential but I never lose sight of the fact that Sandwich, and indeed the whole area, no matter what my dear, dear friends say, is just a little bit out of the way and there isn't really sufficient depth of population to keep the many clubs going full-bore in the winter.

I'm sure many would argue that there are many other courses not nearer big populations, but if you actually take a close look you'll find there are big towns within a train or bus ride and this is simply not the case in the far reaches of Kent. Road communications, although they are improving all the time despite certain cut-backs, just don't quite stretch the extra miles to reach those courses in Kent and many, of course, argue that it is the delightful feeling of remoteness that makes getting away for golf there such fun.

The Prince's course was taken over by Sir Aynsley Bridgeland who came to Britain, so I'm told by a very old chum, with three ambitions: to get down to scratch, to own his own golf club and to get a knighthood. He achieved all three.

Royal St George's, Sandwich

I always look forward to Royal St George's, where the 1981 Open is scheduled after being omitted from the Open rota since 1949, the year Bobby Locke won on a play-off against Irishman Harry Bradshaw, who suffered when his ball finished up in the bottom half of a broken beer bottle. Harry, as we remember, made the mistake of playing the ball where it lay, or felt he was not entitled to relief, and gave the ball a shattering whack without eye damage, but lost the championship by that single stroke. I doubt if we shall ever see anything like this happen again. Today, when a player feels, or knows, he is entitled to a free drop he consults his 'book of rules' but seems never to take the risk of carrying out what he finds there. Instead, play is held up while an official is summoned and confirms whatever it may be that he is allowed to do. Sensible of the player, because he has made quite sure that he cannot be penalised a shot or two because responsibility is firmly on the official's shoulders; but it's tedious for spectators.

Royal St George's, Sandwich: a typical view for competitors in the 1981 Open — but there is a fairway out there somewhere (*Peter Dazeley Photography*)

St George's has enjoyed much fame. Ian Fleming used it as the setting of the match between Bond and Goldfinger for his novel *Goldfinger*, although when the film was shot with Sean Connery in the lead, the golfing sequences were, in fact, filmed at Stoke Poges.

St George's has a marvellous golfing atmosphere — reserved for men only. Everything about it is down to earth with the professional's shop being a real one, not a fashion salon. You can still smell the glue and the leather grips. And there is a battered vice, and a well-worn bench over which have stood customers instructing or watching craftsmen make minor changes to favourite clubs.

For all my support of ladies golf and equal rights for absolutely everybody, I should hate to think that clubs like Royal St George's might ever change. It's full of fiery colonels, wing commanders, generals and significant city types dressed in their thick tweeds and sturdy well-polished brogues. It's a place where you cannot show off, or drop names or pretend, because even if you have won the Victoria Cross, there may be someone there who has a bar to it. If you have £4 million, maybe there is a quiet chap sitting in the corner with a small whisky who has £8 million!

Royal St George's is felt, by some, to be for the rich, famous and titled only. But as is the case at Muirfield, acting the snob — once you're in — is absolutely pointless. The great thing about the place is that once you are a

172

member, you're on an equal footing with everyone, whether you are the local postman or a landowner. It is true that the public school system of addressing people by their surnames is in evidence, but that is how the type of member was brought up. And is there so very much wrong with that?

Part of its charm to me is that the place seemingly ignores the fact that women do exist. There are no ladies tees and I'm told it is true that when one chap arrived with his wife the following conversation, outside the clubhouse, took place. 'Excuse me. Are ladies allowed to play?' The uncertain member said he wasn't sure about ladies 'But I know they allow dogs.'

Some imagine that no big event, even the 1981 Open, will attract large crowds to Royal St George's. Well, despite the approach roads, I wouldn't like to put my meagre life savings on that, for it has been thirty years and more since London last had an Open within a comfortable drive. Some took early bets that it would break all records and if the new roads are clear, and the days are bright, then who knows? What I do know is that the larks, the sandhills, the wild garlic and the wind from the sea make it a special place and when the golf is over for the day you can sit in those very, very old leather chairs in the clubhouse and read through *Country Life*, or *Punch*, have your toasted teacake and maybe play backgammon in the famous window. And while you do this, expect almost anyone to walk into the bar — Hollywood film actors, former Prime Ministers, war heroes.

The best holes for me are the 1st, 15th and 18th. If you manage a 4 at each of these you'll be on top of the world.

Selsdon Park

As a total contrast, let me take you now to Selsdon Park, near Croydon! It has a fine hotel where Harry Weetman, one of my old chums who died in a motor crash, was professional for a number of years. Selsdon Park, a hilly inland course, was the venue of the old Sprite tournament. The sponsors made caravans and our PGA tour pitched there for the tournament one year and I tied with Harold Henning and, I think, Neil Coles. The following year I remember holing in one at the 17th and there was no car as prize, as in the previous year. Maddening!

Although I haven't been to Selsdon for a while, I well remember standing on the huge lawn and looking at the ivy-clad hotel, which really is most impressive. Some years ago they celebrated their 75th birthday with a vast banquet in Henry VIII style, and it went on most of the night. The course isn't tigerish but the set-up, particularly for businessmen who wish to work and play, is first class.

Harry Weetman about to deliver one of the most fearsome blows on the golf scene of the 1950s (*Bert Neale*)

Bangor

My favourites come in no kind of order so let me take you now to Bangor in Northern Ireland, a modest parkland course where I won the Jeyes tournament in the mid-1960s. Even then, a few of the lads used to laugh because I was twitching about on the short putts — but the ball always seemed to go into the hole, maybe by the side or even back door, as we say, but in they went, and I won.

Hoylake

I mentioned the 1947 Open at Hoylake earlier. Father once had an assistant called Dan Thwaite and he became pro at the municipal there and we stayed

174

with him, father, brother and myself. My father, around 54 in those days, still played in a few tournaments. In fact he opened up in the now defunct *News of the World* match-play championship at Hoylake one year against George Duncan; they went round in about two hours and ten minutes, and the old man won by 2 and 1. It was headline stuff, for the sheer speed of the match, and the quality of play.

It was at Hoylake in 1949 that Guy Wolstenholme and I met while serving in the RAF in those parts. Guy Farrar was secretary. We turned up one August day wearing RAF boots and so on. Anyway I took my jacket off, played in those boots and RAF uniform, and Guy says I went round in 67, which would have been very handy in the Open, later in my career. Well that 67 in boots is the story told by Guy, never known to lie and still winning tournaments in Australia in 1980 at the tender age of 49!

You can look out across the flat course from the clubhouse and can feel ghosts of great players past, and think, for instance, of Bobby Jones completing the second leg of his 1930 grand slam of the Open and Amateur championships of both Britain and the USA or those greatest of early amateur golfers who played most of their golf as Hoylake members, Harold Hilton and John Ball. To play the course is always an experience and a particularly testing one in the wind.

(*left*) George Duncan, 1920 Open champion, at 73 in 1957 (*Bert Neale*); (*right*) Harold Hilton. Note that the ball is placed unusually far back in the stance

Bobby Locke and Flory van Donck of Belgium will remember just how tough Hoylake is from their abortive struggles to win the 1956 Open championship there. That was the occasion the wind did blow and howl until sometime after about 3 o'clock when Peter Thomson took his place on the first tee, by which time the wind had dropped, the sun was out, and the rain had stopped.

So Thomson went on to win his third Open in a row. Locke was flooded out (I recall him tipping the water out of his golf bag) and van Donck was pipped at the post, all of which showed how Hoylake can be very cruel indeed. But perhaps no one can have fonder memories than Roberto de Vicenzo. After years of coming close, his victory at Hoylake in the 1967 was one of the most popular of all. Though more often than not he found putting a torture, what a magnificent striker of the ball he was. I've seen no one in my time to better him.

I was sorry to see the course taken off the Open rota, edged out by rising attendances because of the lack of hotels in the area, car-parking and soon. I played my first Open here in Fred Daly's year, 1947.

Moor Park

More memories come floating back whenever people talk about Moor Park, in Hertfordshire. It was at this spot I played in my very first serious event, back in 1946. It was the Carris Trophy and my brother again was chaperone. They always seemed to have fine weather at Moor Park where they opened the professional season with the old Silver King and Spalding tournaments. Invariably it seemed, John Panton used to win, having motored down from Glenbervie, often in the latest Rover car.

I always thought the High Course extremely difficult. The West Course was reduced by many competitors to a brisk 66 which frightened the life out of me. In those days they had the State Express cigarette event and anyone who had three consecutive 3s only one at a par 3 won himself 300 State Express 333 cigarettes, which perhaps heralded the arrival of bigger prizes for holes in one, and so on.

Moor Park in 1964 was the scene of my Esso tournament triumph, probably as good a tournament as ever I played. I hit the ball well and even holed long putts. All seemed well with my world during that tournament. Cameras never seemed to click at the wrong time, spectators kept still and the game of golf was rather easy. It was a round-robin affair where selected players played each other in turn and even before the last round I had won enough points so that nobody could catch me. I lost only one game and that to Christy O'Connor after being one up and two to play and finishing 5,3

176

A homely little clubhouse — Moor Park
(*Peter Dazeley Photography*)

Here I am, playing the best golf of my life
in the Esso Tournament in 1964 at Moor
Park (*Sport & General*)

while he finished 4,2. In another clash Kel Nagle managed to halve with me after finishing with a 2, otherwise I would have had a clean sweep.

Anyway, the setting of the clubhouse is absolutely magnificent and John Jacobs, who was pro over the hill at Sandy Lodge, and myself used to play there and imagine what it was like in the days of Cardinal Wolsey when the servants ate in what are now locker rooms. There were magnificent escape tunnels in case soldiers arrived. The Orange Room, and the main hall must cost the members a fortune to keep warm, and in good condition. But to have a stately home as your clubhouse, with tennis courts thrown in and a fine dining hall where one imagines venison could be served any day, is to be treasured. They used to extend the dining-room into a kind of conservatory during pro tournaments and the press and players used to swop notes and stories in this most splendid clubhouse.

The Orangery is now the pro's shop, presided over by Ross Whitehead. It is the short holes I remember most vividly.

Long Ashton

Our magic carpet takes us now to the West of England and Long Ashton where I tied with Bill Large in a Martini tournament. I remember it well because I was standing behind the 18th green and Bill, now at Potters Bar, wanted a 4 to tie and he pushed his second shot out to the right, leaving a not very easy pitch to the green from about thirty-five yards. He flipped it up to about nine feet and knocked it in to tie, to my utter horror!

Wally Smithers was the pro at Long Ashton for years and was such a character in the game. We used to meet up and celebrate. Ah, those were the days.

The course lay in an area that used to be starved of golf until the Severn Bridge was opened and St Pierre at Chepstow and other courses came into motoring range.

Stoke Poges

But on, this time to another memory and the Stoke Poges course which, I think, has the potential of being the best club north of the river. I've had some good times there, and bad too. I won the Agfa-Gaevert tournament there in 1966, going round in 64 once and it was there, on a slightly different course, that my father beat Mark Seymour in the final of the British Match-Play championship in the mid-1930s. They had the 18th, in those days, as a short hole across a lake but that has been altered now into a testing par 4 with rough up the right-hand side.

Stoke Poges has a pleasant atmosphere and a monster clubhouse which must be cripplingly expensive to look after but is a very interesting building, protected because of its architectural significance. It features in occasional TV films and is always recognised by those of us who know it so well. I believe it has the potential to be one of the best inland courses north of the Thames and the middle section of the second nine is testing indeed.

Little Aston

One of the most beautifully groomed courses in Britain, and another favourite of mine, is Little Aston in the Midlands. Having been brought up at Ferndown, which looked as though it had been prepared with surgical precision, one didn't often see anything as good — and it was certainly a long day's march to see anything better.

Little Aston was really top-class though hardly anyone ever seemed to play there. The stories were that the membership was select but Charlie Ward, one of the top players in Britain just after the war, must have had quite a battle to make a living — perhaps they paid him a huge retainer or he liked the quietness in order to practise his pitching and putting on that wonderful putting green. The first time I saw the green, it almost bowled

(*left*) Charlie Ward, master of putt and chip (*Bert Neale*); (*right*) Bernard Hunt (*Sport & General*)

me over with its heather edges and delightful undulations. It really was a test.

Little Aston has a relatively modest clubhouse with the course considered to be what matters. It was here I won my first tournament the Daks in 1954 and I remember it specially because once again I had to stand behind the 18th green to see if last-man-out Bobby Locke could tie me with a 4. He aimed his drive, as usual, out to the right to allow for his draw — but it didn't come back as expected and clattered into a tree, and that was that. He couldn't reach the green in two, chipped up and missed the putt and the prize was mine.

Incidentally in those days they didn't put the leaders out last; it was luck of the draw and I was out first. We did two rounds, yes two, in three hours and fifty-four minutes. I did 68 and 69 or something like it, and Bernard Hunt, my partner, wasn't much more. Take heed young slow, very slow, maestros.

St Andrews

Memories begin to play tricks with the passing of the years but I think I first saw St Andrews, the Home of Golf, in 1947. It was at a Spalding tournament won by Henry Cotton; a year later Norman von Nida won there, so you can see it produced class winners, and almost always has. Anyway, my father had given my brother £50 to take him and me to three tournaments — just imagine, that for £50.

I had my first taste of St Andrews and thought it fantastic. The town had incredible atmosphere, but it is the Tudor Tearooms I remember particularly well. I was about seventeen and a very pretty waitress served me tea and toast and I plucked up courage to ask her if she'd like to go to the pictures. She agreed, and we held hands. It was the start of a love affair with St Andrews and I made some great friends. Particularly, the Andersons, who live over the top of the hill at Dairsie. He's the past president of the Royal Caledonian Curling Society and they live in a lovely house called Pittormie. A lawyer, a fruit farmer, a quarry owner and a member of the R and A golf club — just a bit of name-dropping really — he's a marvellous man.

St Andrews is where I once put together a 66 of which I'm particularly proud (six 3s and the rest all 4s) and it's where a great chum, Tony Lema of America, won the 1964 Open and later, much to my distress, was killed in a flying accident. The place is golf history, and incident. We saw Kel Nagle win the Centenary Open there, hotly chased by Arnold Palmer. Bobby Locke won there, Peter Thomson and all the great names such as J. H.

(*above*) Norman von Nida (*Keystone Press Agency*); (*right*) Ed Sneed at the 1978 Open at St Andrews just after he had lost a commanding lead in the US Masters (*Michael Hobbs*)

Taylor, James Braid, Sam Snead, Jack Nicklaus and Bobby Jones. St Andrews has seen them all.

Maybe the course is overplayed by holiday-makers but it earns money for the town so it is very difficult to shut up shop in the grass-growing season. I love it and I'm sure every golfer who respects the game loves it equally as much.

St Andrews is held in such respect that many think it should permanently house the Open championship, rather as Wembley always hosts the FA Cup final, Twickenham the home of England rugby internationals, Wimbledon the world's pre-eminent tennis Open and so on.

Actually I think that ideally one should have four venues for the Open and it is a great pity, politically, that one cannot have it in England, Ireland, Scotland and Wales, which would be a superb way of doing it. Yet you might play it on more than four links because in Scotland you cannot imagine ignoring Muirfield in favour of St Andrews. Then you will get complaints from the Carnoustie supporters — and what about Turnberry which produced such a wonderful championship with that famous finish between Watson and Nicklaus?

Wales, of course, has Royal Porthcawl, a great setting. England has Royal Birkdale, Royal Lytham, Royal St George's, while Ireland has marvellous courses in both north and south, in Royal Portrush and Portmarnock.

I'm always amazed to hear of American professionals who have learned to play the game astonishingly well despite being unaware of the qualities of St Andrews. It is almost as though their education is incomplete. But when we sit here thinking about all the things we have going for us, it is easy to forget that Americans can find almost perpetual sunshine, even though they may have to fly and motor a bit across the States for it. Many Americans are at a complete loss when they tackle St Andrews but until you have played the Old Course, and played it well, you are, in many ways, not a complete golfer.

When you walk down the last fairway, seemingly almost into the very town itself, you get a wonderful feeling that all the golfers, from ages past, are walking with you. And when the grandstands are full, it can be an unforgettable experience. It possibly unsettled Doug Sanders when he needed a 4 to win the Open but if you had to choose a hole on which to score a 4 to win, you wouldn't look much further than the last at St Andrews, even more so for a player of his calibre. The fairway is 150 yards wide with not a bunker in sight — it's a drive and a short pitch for the simple 4. But

(*opposite*) Sam Snead, perhaps at his peak in the late 1940s. He won the 1946 Open at St Andrews

183

(*left*) Clubhouse and 18th green at Muirfield (*Peter Dazeley Photography*)

(*below*) The bridge over the Swilcan burn, St Andrews. The burn runs across the 1st and last fairways (*Peter Dazeley Photography*)

tragically Sanders took 5 and every time I see him miss the putt from three feet six inches on a TV re-play I think he can't possibly miss it again! But he always does, on the same right-hand side. In a way it was all the more tragic for Sanders because he must have felt he had won the championship after he had found that feared bunker at the side of the Road Hole (17th) and had then played what had seemed an impossibly delicate bunker shot to the side of the hole to get his par. Indeed some who were there that day round the 18th claim that it was not Sanders's putting that let him down but his approach shot. All through the championship he had been playing run-up shots to the greens but this last time decided to pitch it full to the flag, hit it a little thin, and there he was at the back of the green with a long putt to come.

Sanders never had another real chance to win the title, although he put up a tremendous fight in the play-off. All we professionals can say when a huge title eludes such a man is 'Bad luck' but that seems totally inadequate. Sanders had been a strong supporter of British golf, quite apart from his adventures on the American tour, where his curtailed and unusual swing won him thousands of dollars.

This drama goes straight into every golf history book and the story will be told, and retold — maybe more accurately and often than the story of how some others actually *won* the title.

I feel the great holes are the 4th, 6th, 13th and, of course, the 17th, the Road Hole, which demands one of the straightest and most correctly weighted second shots in golf. Yet two of the easiest holes in golf — the 1st and 18th — linger as strongly in the memory, mainly because of the atmosphere given them by the town huddling around.

Royal Lytham and St Anne's

On to another championship course, Royal Lytham and St Anne's, where I had some success, winning the Dunlop tournament in 1959 with a score of 280. It was there that I first met Cliff Michelmore who was doing some TV interviews. I had my son Gary with me at the time and Cliff asked my bright five-year-old offspring what he wanted to do when he grew up. Did he want to follow in Grand-dad's footsteps, or in Dad's footsteps? Gary said he didn't. He just wanted to follow in the steps of the Lone Ranger. This let the Alliss family down with a bump, but gave us all a good laugh.

However, Gary went on to create a niche in the golf world. He didn't start until he was 17, which maybe left it a bit late for entering world-wide professional golf on the playing side, but after starting his apprenticeship at Trevose, down in north Cornwall, he moved on to be assistant with John

Bob Charles's swing has always been considered a little awkward but I suspect that a left-hander merely looks 'different' (*Peter Dazeley*)

(*opposite*) Tony Jacklin just before he won the Open (*Colorsport*)

Cook at the East Berks Golf Club, which is near Camberley and in the spring of 1979 took his first full professional's job at Harpenden, in Hertfordshire, where he is enjoying life to the full, and a good golf professional he is, I'm very proud to say.

Lytham is one of my favourite championship courses. It's compact and I liken it to the Grand National because the favourites come and go, but you never really know who is going to win, or who is going to fall. It's thrown up some interesting winners. You could argue that Bob Charles and the fellow he tied with, Phil Rodgers, were not the two best players in that particular field. But the exam paper was set, and they came out on top.

It was at Lytham that David Thomas tied with Peter Thomson in 1958 and how near he came to winning, just hitting his second shot at the 71st hole with a 7-iron that bit heavy, finishing three or four yards short and taking three more to get down for a 5. So his life was changed because if

186

he'd won that day, things would have been different, just as, I suspect, Tony Jacklin's future was affected by Trevino in the 1972 Open at Muirfield, holing all manner of shots, including a thinned one from a bunker that clattered the flag and plummetted down and in, during the third round, and then in the last round, with Jacklin poised to go into the lead on the 71st, holing a chip shot for one of the most unlikely par 5s I've ever seen. To have won there would, I think, have put aside any last doubts that Tony might have had that he was a great player and that perhaps two Opens in less than a year might have been a brief flash of supreme form. True, David Thomas's achievements had been a class lower but he had one superb repetitive shot that meant in any tournament he was always there with a chance: he was for a good spell the longest *straight* driver in the world.

The wind at Lytham makes a great difference. Although it's an enclosed circuit, you have the railway on the right, and houses on the other side as you play the inward nine — it's not really claustrophobic, because it has wonderful holes which keep your mind on the job in hand. If you've the wind with you going out, you must take advantage of this and get out in 33 shots at worst, because the inward half suddenly becomes a monster.

The clubhouse has a marvellous feeling about it with its wide, wooden staircase up to the panelled landing and passages. Not far away is the

The clubhouse at Royal Lytham (*Peter Dazeley Photography*)

putting green, on to which you almost fall as you leave the main entrance, and a few yards away a pro shop tucked in the corner. There's a dormy house not far away. The club serves fine food and there are rows of pictures of old club captains. You can find a good, leather chair and even a brass barometer. All so typical of the best in British clubhouses, and I love it.

I always go to Lytham with a keen sense of anticipation, perhaps partly because it is all so close to the hustle and bustle of Blackpool — absolutely another world. It was there I first stayed with my friend Justin Rickard, whose family have run the Headlands Hotel on the South Shore so successfully for many years, a really splendid establishment.

The course starts with an attractive 3 and for me some of the best holes are the underestimated ones: 2nd, 8th, 10th, 13th and 16th. And the 18th has been the downfall of a few potential winners.

Carnoustie

Quite a different kettle of fish is Carnoustie. I played there in 1953, the year the great Ben Hogan won and well remember the crowds galloping after the great man the only time he played in the Open championship. It would have done credit to a Hollywood movie. The links is an extraordinary place. It's rather ugly in parts with a railway siding and the low group of houses close to the 18th hole. Over the years it has been developed and there is a brand new clubhouse.

There is a strange feature at Carnoustie, which seems to exist at more and more clubs in Scotland in that there isn't what could be called a full club professional. There isn't one at Muirfield or St Andrews either. Several clubs have playing rights over the course, which actually belongs to the town.

David Thomas and our golf construction company have been concerned with the building of a second course, which runs alongside the sea-side of the championship course and, given a trouble-free run, it could be a fine test.

Not everyone loves Carnoustie. Southerners tend to think the place bleak and on a windy day, even a good professional is hard pushed to break 80. Well, I can vouch for that. The course is more than 7,000 yards long and a challenge it most certainly is. Hogan won by four shots, improving on his score with every round with 73, 71, 70, 68. Dai Rees, yet again, was one of the runners-up.

Hogan never returned for a British Open. I often wondered why. Perhaps he didn't think much of us, although he has mentioned his Carnoustie triumph as one of his biggest thrills. I believe he didn't at all relish our

(*left*) Hogan about to rule an iron shot on the flag at Carnoustie, 1953 (*Bert Neale*); (*right*) Hogan returns: Wentworth, Canada Cup, 1956 (*Bert Neale*)

weather and found the greens too slow for his taste. I think he only played in Britain once more, at Wentworth in the 1956 Canada Cup (later the World Cup). Most of the photographs you see of him in British golf magazines and books were taken on that occasion when it seemed that just about every spectator followed Hogan and Snead.

Incidentally my best round there in the Open was a 71 and in that year I had a total of 292 and, although quite a way behind Mr Hogan, there weren't a great number of players between us!

If Muirfield is the fairest Open course, I think Carnoustie can rank as the most difficult. The 6th is as good a par 5 as you can find anywhere and the 17th and 18th are very formidable. The 7th should be lengthened and the 8th tee realigned. Opinions differ on the 16th and personally I dislike it: a very long shot to a slightly domed green requires luck as well as power and skill and certainly in Opens it plays to a par of about 3½.

Turnberry

Turnberry, the most recent links to be included on the Open championship list, was a favourite place of my dear friend Henry Longhurst. He used to sit on the verandah outside the hotel, perched high above the course with the lighthouse in the distance, and scan the sea to Ailsa and across to the high peak of Goat Fell on the isle of Arran. On a wild day one could imagine how hard it must have been to get an aircraft off the old airstrip which the course was in two world wars.

What a magnificent thing that Turnberry was resurrected for golfers after the runways had done their bit though it's still possible to make use of one on the Arran course to hit the longest drive of your life. Your ball may bound along for 500 yards but, alas, out of bounds all the way.

Those who know the Ailsa course at Turnberry rightly regard it as an absolute delight and what splendid views it has. However, when it comes on to blow or rain, one seems invariably at the far end of the course, almost out to sea by the lighthouse itself. Who can ever forget the grandstand finish to the 1977 Open which, for the last two rounds, become a match-play battle between Jack Nicklaus and Tom Watson? It was a rare treat, vintage stuff with these two men 'lapping' the field many shots ahead of the third-place

Tom Watson *(Bert Neale)*

man, and ending the week with birdies each. Nicklaus from right across the green and Watson from a couple of feet, having that putt to win.

Again, my company had been called in to alter the course but unfortunately only about a quarter of our ideas were used, due, mainly to a question over money. I'm sure the R and A were not at fault, but British Transport Hotels couldn't, at that time, see that the expenditure would be justified. Even so only the two leaders broke par — and they crucified it with 268, but the third man, Hubert Green, certainly didn't tear the course to bits, nor did anyone else.

But you must breathe that Turnberry air, and wander down to Bob Jamieson's shop and get the feel of the place. No wonder Henry loved it so dearly — we all do. The potential is there in terms of terrain and scenery to make it the greatest golf course in the world and I consider that it should be made a tigerish test without regard to the punishment it might inflict on high handicappers.

Blairgowrie

For years I had heard about Blairgowrie (Rosemount) and again our company had the opportunity to build a new course there. It is a famous part of the world, though cursed with a really icy winter. But it has silver birch, pine and heather and the setting is beautiful. I went there first to play with David Thomas in the old Sumrie Four-ball, and was delighted with it all.

The new course has come on in leaps and bounds and has already staged the Scottish championship and it may well go from strength to strength.

At that time the secretary was Bob Malcolm, now retired, and what a splendid fellow he was. A great deal of golf is played there each year and the takings in green fees alone are remarkable, especially considering that much of the season is lost because of the fierceness of the winter, with snow and ice holding on until late spring sometimes.

Walton Heath

Now, quickly, let's jump on our jet and fly down south to Walton Heath, another wild stretch of country, a genuine heathland course which has changed its character several times, even since I've known it. Heather and silver birch abound along the edges of many fairways but also there is an immense growth of ferns which, although they've been cut back, still grow with vigour.

Walton Heath remains one of Surrey's most memorable courses and is

Winner of the 1980 European Open at Walton Heath, Tom Kite (*Michael Hobbs*)

back now into big-time golf. It was here that the first *News of the World* match-play championship was played after the war and it was here, too, that my father reached the final, only to be beaten by the then little-known player Reg Horne. Dad, a fifty-year-old at the time, put up a good show indeed against Horne, a superb practice-round player and a super striker of the ball who should have won more tournaments than he did.

Well, I knew nothing of Walton Heath in those days and when I did come face to face with it, I was quite terrified to see five feet high ferns, and heather like wire wool all waiting to collect anything even a fraction off-line. But to compensate there was marvellous fairway turf to hit the ball from.

Having enjoyed my friendship with Cliff Michelmore, which goes back to 1959, it was a delight to find he had a house in nearby Reigate. And so he, and his dear wife Jean Metcalfe, invited me to stay there and I became known as 'the fat lodger'. No wonder, because she is a wonderful cook and they kept a wondrous cellar.

Walton Heath has a long history, with memories of James Braid as professional for decades and later came Harry Busson, a fine club-maker and no mean player. Great interest was shown in the club by Sir William Carr, one-time proprietor of the *News of the World*, who used to play often with Henry Cotton. Now they have one of the master secretaries in the world of golf, ex-RAF officer and Irish international, Bill McCrae. He has worked long and hard to rejuvenate the club and the reward came when the European Open went there, and the Ryder Cup match itself. There is the problem of a busy road but when a composite course is made up for tournaments that is eliminated.

Royal Porthcawl

This club in South Wales was the scene of my father's first professional job. He went there as assistant in about 1919. I first came across the course while representing the Bournemouth Alliance in a home and away fixture that we had with the South Wales Alliance in those far-off days.

I remember doing the journey many times from Bournemouth to Porthcawl with an old friend and former English Amateur champion, Ernest Millward, sadly no longer with us. We used to stay at the South Beach Hotel, battered by wind and sea spray, with the Knipe brothers — both fair players, one professional and one amateur. The drive from the town up to the golf course passed a huge, satanic building on the right, which turned out to be a rest home for coal miners suffering from those

Max Faulkner with that billiard cue and driftwood putter (*Bert Neale*)

feared chest complaints associated with mining. Just looking at it made one appreciate one's health and strength and being involved in such a game as golf, which took one out into God's fresh air.

You had only to stand and look across the course to appreciate its raw, natural beauty. The course has a broad sweep to it and if it hasn't been captured on canvas, it ought to be.

The opening holes by the sea are unforgettable and in my day Wally Gould starred as the professional. It had a quaint clubhouse, made of wood and iron, and they served tea in slievers — big mugs with silver handles — as you sat in front of a stove reading the magazines which looked as though they had been there for years.

The pro shop sold everything: packets of chewing gum, shoe laces, woolly hats and you could smell the varnish and feel the history of the place. It was the real thing and Wally was from a long line of golf professionals, with his brother Harold just a little bit further down the road, at Southerndown, another excellent course.

As I mentioned, it was father's first job. It had been a toss-up as to whether he would take it, or have a trial for the Yorkshire County Cricket Club. Well, the letter from Porthcawl came first and so off he went, as assistant to Mr Hutchinson.

I have made two *A Round with Alliss* programmes there, with 1951 Open winner Max Faulkner and Welsh entertainer Max Boyce. I always feel at home here at Wales's answer to Royal Lytham.

Royal Troon

Another famous seaside course is Troon, now happily back on the Open rota. It was here I had one of my best golfing days. I was with a journalist chum, Bob Ferrier, and a cartoonist named Iain Reid and we were doing the forerunner to a golf-instruction strip cartoon. It was in the early 1960s, shortly after Arnold Palmer's Open win. The course was in tip-top condition, a contrast to the dust-bowl it had been for the Open in July 1962. It was a spring day, the kind which made the heart leap.

I remember the fairways were tight and green, it was a one-pullover day, we had caddies, the greens had been beautifully cut and we talked about the golf cartoon which, sadly for me, wasn't to be. But it was to make some worthwhile money for the young Gary Player.

The Royal Troon clubhouse, made of solid stone, and one of my favourite hotels, the Marine just a stroll away, make a grand setting. Margaret McChristie, the superb lady who has been everything in the hotel from chief cook, and bottle-washer, to the receptionist has now gone but she will

Arnold Palmer drives from the 18th tee at Augusta, 1970. You can almost feel the power in that right hand

Johnny Miller who came near to winning the 1973 Open at Troon (*Peter Dazeley Photography*)

be remembered. Archie, the head waiter moved on — things change — but it was a day when all was right with the world.

The little 8th, the 'Postage Stamp' gave Gene Sarazen a 1 and 2 on consecutive days and Palmer a terrible time the same year but perhaps the 11th is the most tigerish hole and I like the way the 18th finishes against the clubhouse.

The Continent of Europe must come in for a mention. If you cross the channel, you can find many marvellous courses which have their own particular air of opulence and grandeur. My first port of call would be El Prat near Barcelona, cursed now by an airport, but it is where I won, and my fortunes changed, in 1956.

El Prat

I was married, had a son, and about £200 to my name when first I went out to this magnificent course at the beginning of the Costa del Sol and I found it superb, although relatively new. Umbrella pines bordered the fairways, which were in spanking condition. Sadly those pines are now dying off, probably because of the tremendous number of aircraft flying overhead and sending down burned-away kerosene, or whatever it is one smells. Let's hope they find a cure for that because El Prat, without the pines, would not be the same.

Varese

I had won, and that seemed to send me on my way. Two years later saw a great burst of Alliss activity as I started off for Varese, in northern Italy, another new course. It was the end of the season and I hadn't been doing too well. I went with my chum Ken Bousfield, who had been enjoying a good year, so I thought it sensible to suggest we pool our resources and see what we could do.

Well Alfonse Angelini had just gone there as professional for a big retainer and he was a terrific man, not in stature but in heart. He'd fought during the war on the Russian front and had lost a few toes from his right foot. But what a good performer he was: fine striker, a good putter and a delightful sense of humour. Well, would you believe, I won that championship by ten strokes? A very nice beginning to a brief tour so on we went to Madrid, to compete at the course where the rich of that great city play.

Puerto de Hierro

Puerto de Hierro boasted fourteen professionals there in those days, and hundreds of caddies. All the members seemed to be dukes or counts and smoked cigarettes with long ivory holders, and filtered as well. They also refused to put their arms into their camel-haired overcoats, resting them on their shoulders and in those days I thought this rather risqué and a method reserved solely for the ladies of Paris.

I thought Wentworth was smart, but I'd never seen such opulence as existed at this Spanish club. It had marble halls, and Turkish towels in the showers, barrels of talcum powder, sweet-smelling hair oil, combs in fine jars of antiseptic everywhere, weighing machines, piles of razors ready to be used by the members and even slippers made out of brown paper so that, after your showers, the feet were not contaminated on the immaculately kept thick pile carpet of the locker room. Golf in Europe is indeed different and there are all the smells of subtle cooking that mean good living.

It was an eye-opener for a young man. I played rather well and won that

(*opposite*) The Alliss swing today (*Peter Dazeley Photography*)

Spanish Open by ten strokes, including a round of 62, but I hasten to add that this was before the course was altered into the giant it is now. But 62, or ten under par, was some going and I was again the winner and on we pressed to the final championship of the year, the Portuguese Open, thoroughly flushed with success.

Estoril

I remember flying into Lisbon and being driven to that beautiful resort, admiring the fine architecture, the horse-drawn cabs, the shoeshine boys, and on to the Palacio Hotel which wasn't quite so grand and plush as it is now. Across the way was the Casino and a little bit further on the clubhouse, among the trees. And in the entrance hall so many coloured birds fluttered around the place that you were advised to keep your hat on!

Once again I won the championship, but this time only by four strokes. I was beginning to weaken! Interesting, because I didn't feel in the slightest bit tired and felt that if the tournament season had gone on it would have been a complete waste of time for anyone else to compete. I was feeling so good that I surely would have gone on winning for ever. It was all mine, three Opens in a row and fifty under par for twelve rounds of golf, which was quite staggering.

I then had to share my loot with my dear friend Ken Bousfield because, as I said, we'd agreed this at the outset and the grand total was about £1,200. By the time we'd taken our expenses off, I actually went home with about £380 profit, but still felt like a millionaire.

I often try to analyse what I did right in that spell. The truth was my putting was steady, I didn't miss many short ones and holed a few long ones. The ball was being driven straight and far, and many top Americans, Billy Casper in particular, consider the drive and putt the two most important shots in golf. Ben Hogan went even further by saying the drive itself is *the* most important. I was knocking them straight, and that probably was the key, though even so an iron is the club from many tees at Estoril.

Worthing

Talking about long driving reminds me of the Worthing golf club, in Sussex. It's a delightful downland stretch where I actually won a long driving competition in 1949. Tom Haliburton set up his world record there of 126 for the first two rounds of a tournament, but the long driving was the memory for me and in the tournament proper I remember hitting the first green a par 4, in one!

Ken Bousfield in 1956 (*Bert Neale*)

Edgar Boone was the professional there; now retired he is, I believe, a director of the club. I always enjoy it there, and the people, and the marvellous views. It was the first downland course I ever played and still recall my surprise at seeing a beach made up of *pebbles*.

Royal Birkdale

However, on we go and Royal Birkdale, at Southport in Lancashire, rates high with me. I first went there in 1954 when Peter Thomson of Australia won his first Open championship. He went for a ten-footer on the last green, missed it and simply lent across on one foot and tapped it in, backhanded, to win with a score of 283.

It was in that championship that I played some of my best Open golf, finishing four strokes behind without holing too many putts. After two rounds, Bill Spence, the club professional from Dartmouth in those days, was leading with scores of 69 and 72. I played with him for the last two

201

The 9th tee at Royal Birkdale (*Peter Dazeley Photography*)

rounds and went 71 and 70 and somehow thought I should have been a lot better, particularly as I had taken 74 in the second round.

I've always had a soft spot for Birkdale, and the Southport area. One of my dearest friends, Freddie Wormold, lives in the end house, separating Royal Birkdale and Hillside golf clubs, and is my 'landlord' when I'm in that area. How lucky I am with my 'private' accommodation. We met some thirty-five years ago when I played at the North Manchester golf club where they staged the Brand Lochryn tournament in, maybe, 1948. I had a rust-coloured jersey which I left with some other things in the dressing-room and Fred recognised them, put them in a parcel and sent them to me, and we've been friends ever since.

Birkdale itself might benefit from one or two alterations to the course. The sixth hole I'm sure could be improved and an alteration to it would detract in no way from the overall picture the course presents.

To me it is the best venue for the Open: car-parking is right by the course, there are hotels in plenty, it is central to the country. Unfortunately spectator movement could be better.

The sweet and difficult holes are the 8th, 10th, 11th (a most testing 4) and the 18th — again right under the clubhouse windows.

Moor Allerton

Until 1980 my home was at Moor Allerton, where Howard Clark is now tournament professional and Peter Blaze the club pro, a few miles north of the centre of Leeds. Opened in 1971, it was here that Robert Trent Jones, certainly the world's highest paid golf-course architect, created his one course in Britain. As such, it is worth a little detail, for it is not well known to southerners.

A lot of money was spent on off-course facilities so that, for example, there are excellent rooms for snooker and table tennis, sauna, leather Chesterfields in all directions and large bars and locker rooms. The restaurant has cuisine of excellent standard rather than the usual homely but plain golf club fare.

However, back to Mr Jones. The course features many of his trade marks. There are the familiar vast undulating greens, flanked by contour-hugging bunkers and, unusual for Britain, much use had been made of ponds and small lakes which come significantly into play at about half-a-dozen holes. It has been argued recently by *The Observer's* Peter Dobereiner that one reason for US golfing superiority is that the free use of water hazards fronting and flanking greens there tempers the will of the US golfer — there's no recovery from water; it's always a shot gone. The greens themselves are very holding so that even the long-handicap golfer at times can imagine he's emulating the pros as he sees his iron shots bite and spin back.

It's a great place for a society outing because the 27-hole layout with the 1st, 10th and 19th starting from the clubhouse means that the field can be dispatched in all directions very quickly. In the future, I think it must come on to the tournament circuit for it is certainly a fine test.

I prefer the 10th to the 27th and single out the 14th, 15th, 18th, 25th and 26th as best holes.

Alwoodley

Nearby Alwoodley is another superb golf course, just down the road from my old house. Although I have to admit if you designed a course like it today, you'd be hanged, drawn and quartered. Over the years, back tees have been put in which means driving over other fairways which might appear a risky business. But if you are not concerned with staging big tournaments, what does it matter? It means waiting a few minutes for other members to play away. It isn't like trying to organise it so 10,000 spectators can all see their heroes.

I was stationed at RAF Catterick during my service days in 1949 and used

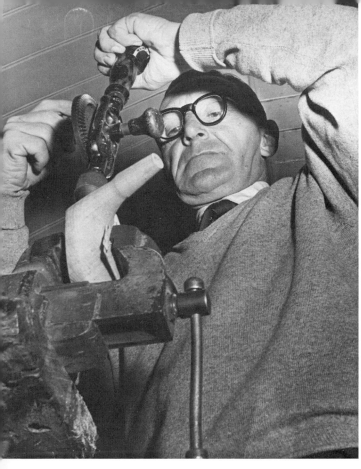
A craftsman at work

to come down to the Leeds area and play golf with Walter Barnes, the son of Ted, professional at Sandmoor and their assistant Ted Docray. We used to play that course, and Moortown, so it's part of the world that had great memories and, before the war my father was professional at the Temple Newsome course, a 36-hole municipal which was torn asunder by open-cast coal mining. But it is now back to being a busy and thriving commercial proposition.

Alwoodley is the epitome of a golf club. Nothing fancy but you get the club, the course, a drink and, if ordered, food. The professional, well, who should it be but Ian Duncan, son of the fabled George. He's got a small wooden shop and maybe feels big-time golf has passed him by, which is a pity because Ian is one of the old type of professionals and some, like me, think the breed marvellous while others think they should make way for the younger ones.

Anyway it's nice to see a man able to practise his club-making trade with efficiency, speed and knowledge. I shall always treasure my conversations with him over the years.

Portmarnock

And while on the subject of speed we must get aboard our magic carpet again and look in at Portmarnock, Eire, where I've stayed with the great Joe Carr on occasions. What a marvellous life he appeared to have. A thriving business, a large family, a character, living on the edge of a golf course — in fact overlooking the Sutton golf club where he had floodlighting put up so he could practise the short game in the dark hours.

Portmarnock has, over the years, staged the Canada Cup, later called the World Cup, and the Carrolls Irish Open. They've done road-widening and alterations but it's still a bit of a nightmare when they all turn up on a Sunday afternoon to watch their champions. Harry Bradshaw, the professional, makes every visit worthwhile. He used to play three rounds a day and, being slightly overweight and suffering from a bit of foot trouble, that was really quite a feat!

When Harry was well past fifty he still used to pull a trolley in some tournaments when he couldn't get a caddie and even at the end of a long day, if a 'punter' appeared, Harry has been known to put a few clubs in a bag and carry for himself in an attempt to win a tenner. What a delightful character. I recall his finish against Dick Mayer in that winning 1957 Ryder Cup side at Lindrick. Mayer had hit the green at the long par-3 last hole and Harry was well short but out came his favourite sand iron and he lobbed it up close and that was a half.

Down the road and you'll find Woodbrook where we used to stay at the International Hotel, Bray, for the Irish Hospitals Sweepstakes event. Just mentioning this brings back a flood of memories of the wild nights and fun.

But Woodbrook doesn't compare with some of the other Irish 'greats' like Ballybunion on the west coast. Now that course really is something spectacular!

I rate Portmarnock as one of the great courses of Europe, fully equipped to test an Open field though lacking good access.

Penina

I once played a Shell match at Penina, a course in the Algarve, designed by Henry Cotton on a ricefield and although it originally looked a disaster, the trees have grown up over the years and now, although it's very long and one has to walk its full distance, even if you play from the forward tees as everything is 'ahead of you' it really is excellent with its majestic hotel, rather like a raised version of Turnberry, overlooking the course. The black swans that sail around greens at spectacular short holes are a feature.

Although they had what is termed 'a bloodless revolution' there not so

Henry Cotton, now an elder statesman of the game (*Bert Neale*)

long ago, Henry and his wife 'Toots' skipped across the border into Spain, almost under cover of darkness, where they spent some time at the new Sotogrande course. But, when things settled down in Portugal they went back and found things, almost certainly, somewhat different.

Cotton, of course, has been an enormous influence on the world of European golf. His enthusiasm is boundless and his efforts on behalf of the young have, on occasions, led to interesting headlines about building hand strength by hitting motor-car tyres and so on, but isn't it marvellous that Cotton should give his time and energy to trying to help. The fact that people were always visiting him kept Penina always busy and, all in all, it's a course that Cotton made.

Sotogrande

Incidentally, if you do find yourself over the border and into Spain, I recommend a visit to Sotogrande which still has that quiet air of luxury, like a more elegant and updated Swinley Forest. David Thomas and I opened it with an exhibition match in the mid-1960s and the course, in those days, was easily reached from Gibraltar. One could fly into the old Rock and pop over the border to the course itself, just twenty minutes in the car. Who knows, this may happen again when the border between Spain and Gibraltar is opened again.

I'd never seen Robert Trent Jones's courses until the mid-1960s and he has built a considerable number in that Costa del Sol stretch and I really don't understand why he made his greens so vast and so sloping, rather like a Picasso interpretation of someone's face. Well, that's the way Trent Jones thinks golf courses should be, and it is difficult to argue with his tremendous success.

Bruntsfield

Memories of travel are great fun, and I look back as far as 1946 and the Boys' championship where, for me, it all started at Bruntsfield, Scotland. It is a fine parkland course and one I shall think about all my life. We went on the night train, my father and I travelling to Edinburgh and I had never

Alliss and David Thomas opening the Atalaya Park Hotel Golf Club on the Costa del Sol (*Bert Neale*)

been so far from home in my life. Having been brought up in the war years, travel was restricted.

I managed to reach the semi-final and was then beaten by a lad almost half my size, Donald Dunsdon. I shall never forget the wonderful write-ups in the newspapers. Willie Allison, the famous Scottish writer who was also the personal PR man to Rangers Football Club, gave me such glowing praise and Leonard Crawley, who wrote for *The Daily Telegraph* in those days and really knew golf inside out, regarded my swing very highly and thought I was destined for great things.

The Boys' winner that year was R. F. D. McGregor, a huge chap of about six foot four inches who wore blue shorts and had legs like telegraph poles.

With Dalmahoy, it's the best course in the immediate area of Edinburgh and has been much improved in recent years.

Dalmahoy

On the other side of Edinburgh you'll find Dalmahoy, a 36-hole complex which has been reorganised over the years, is a great place to stage a professional tournament, and a course which I hope will remain on the PGA list for many years. In a region with a wealth of courses, this is still very much worth a visit.

Lindrick

Let's look in now at Lindrick, scene of the 1957 Ryder Cup match. The times John Jacobs and I stayed there in the days of the good old Sir Stuart Goodwin Foursomes days were happy, and more so because John's mother was the stewardess there for many years. How well I remember her huge breakfasts: the kidney, bacon, tomatoes, the mushrooms, the sausages, the fried bread, the sweetbreads. Bliss!

It's odd to think how many good courses have major roads running through them and Lindrick is no exception, although during the Ryder Cup matches it was closed to all traffic.

Lindrick has a gentle, but toughish opening hole. Out of bounds on the left makes it a hole at which you are always pleased to open with a 4. It has a funny little drive-and-pitch 2nd hole, a sort of dogleg right to left, and then a good short hole, and then on you go finishing up right in front of the club-house with a longish short hole. Here again it's no detriment to finish with a short hole, although many designers seem to frown on this. Another course that finishes with a short hole is Moor Park, which, in a tight finish, can produce tremendous excitement.

208

Swinley Forest

Although I've only played it a couple of times, I love Swinley Forest. I went there some time ago with a dear friend, also sadly no longer with us, Andrew Hughes-Onslow, who was a five-day member of this miniature Sunningdale. The smallish clubhouse, which boasted superb food, had an air of days gone by and if you didn't feel privileged to be there, well, you shouldn't have been asked to come.

The Earl of Derby owns the land and there used to be tales of the members sitting around at the end of the year to decide what it had cost to run the club. Then the total was divided up among the members, who were all billed accordingly. Whether that's true or not, I don't know. But if that system works, then it's not such a bad idea. Hard on the pocket if the clubhouse roof collapses though. It reminds me of an American club with a similar system. A member might say that the 13th could do with a lake fronting the green; that the locker room was too small; that there was nowhere to have a quiet game of cards. The president of the club was apt to take heed and the work would be carried out. The member would then be presented with the bill. There were fewer complaints about course and clubhouse there than at most clubs!

Burnham and Berrow

Burnham and Berrow, in Somerset, is a place you must visit. It was there I won the Burnham and Berrow Winter Foursomes with my old friend from Ferndown days, that publican I've told you about, Bob Hill. We used to motor over every two weeks, on a Sunday, and play, at first light, in the early 1950s. His wife came from that area and her brother, Jack Pool, was a very staunch Somerset player along with Jack Payne, George Irlam and many more and it reminds me now of the number of very good players there were in that area in those days, thirty years ago.

Gleneagles

Gleneagles has fond memories for me, stretching back right into the Alliss archives. My father won the Scottish Open there around 1935 with a score of 266 and the championship wasn't played again until Graham Marsh won the resurrected tournament in the mid-1970s, so Dad was perhaps the longest-reigning Open champion of all time.

Marsh, incidentally, won his championship at St Andrews. It has always seemed strange to me that Scotland, which virtually gave the world the game of golf (even though the Dutch, with their kolven, and, possibly,

209

Julius Caesar might argue) should not have a proper 'Open championship' every year. But then, perhaps, that might clash too strongly with the championship.

Gleneagles is now the home of pro-celebrity golf on TV and while the superb hotel struggles with inflation, it goes on and God forbid that anything should happen to it because it could never be replaced. The staff are a marvellous breed and it always thrills me to motor down the drive, past Ian Marchbanks's pro shop where Derek Brown presides so well, past the homely dormy house and new Log Cabin bar where super food is served at very reasonable prices.

If you haven't been to Perthshire, you really must take my word and go. Courses like Gleneagles, when in good condition, are an unforgettable experience. Sadly, some of them, get overplayed and recently two bad winters have taken their toll. But Scotland is full of grand courses, and we cannot mention them all.

My choice of the best 18 here would include the first 10 holes of the Queen's course and the first 8 of the King's. The most challenging holes are the 4th, 8th, 13th and 17th.

Graham Marsh (*Peter Dazeley Photography*)

A typical scene at Gleneagles (*Peter Dazeley Photography*)

Maesdu

Wales, too, has many fine courses. Maesdu, at Llandudno, for holiday golf, is well known. It was in 1957, and the week that I went with my brother to take up the position at Parkstone that I left him there to play in the PGA championship, and six days later I was back again, with the cup itself.

So Maesdu, for me, will always have happy memories particularly as I won there twice. I remember coming down the 18th hole, needing a 5 to win. There's an out of bounds on the right by the practice ground and if you go wildly to the right, you're in the hospital. Well, I aimed it so far left, because the wind was whistling from that direction, that I almost went out of bounds across the second, way off-course. Anyway, I battled down the fairway, and eventually won it, with a 5.

Tom Jones used to be professional at Maesdu and, for many years, was a top official of the PGA and I can see his marvellously craggy and kindly face now, with his almost permanent smile always flickering there and, with his fine tenor voice, his delight in singing those stirring, patriotic Welsh songs.

Killarney

Once more, quickly, we must dash over the water to include Killarney in Ireland amongst my favourites. Tony Coveney, one-time assistant to Henry Cotton, has been there many years. Go and look, and savour the views. Remember that there is a grand book about Lord Castleross, whose family was so embedded in this area. Look at the lake and get the feeling of the Irish magic. It's sheer delight. A strange course, maybe, with a mixture of waterside holes, and inland. But it's unforgettable.

The 18th, a par 3 of 200 yards plus is one of the most memorable holes in golf. There's the lake on the right and rhododendron bushes to the left and a few pines between the edge of the green and the water. Clearly, it offers one of the most satisfying achievements in golf: a full shot with wood or long iron that soars, hangs against the sky and then plunges to the green — or maybe you slice into water or pull and hook into the rhododendrons which then rapidly lose their charm. And if you come in soaked to the skin from the not unusual downpours they will nod and agree that it's a 'soft day'.

Westward Ho!

So many great courses to see. Westward Ho! in north Devon is where J. H. Taylor was brought up and where you'll find golf as it used to be played, with the dreaded needles out there, a kind of fierce rush which traps any misdirected shot. It is sad that it is a bit out of the way, for few tournaments are staged there, although it makes for a splendid holiday, along with nearby Saunton.

At St Enedoc, north Cornwall, somebody once took a deep divot, hit a bit of stone, dug down with his hands, and before you could say Trebetherick, had discovered a church that had lain buried under the sand dunes for years and years.

212

There are so many courses and stories I should have mentioned. There are so many places I haven't seen such as Nairn, or Royal Dornoch, to which Ben Crenshaw, with his fine sense of golf history, made a pilgrimage just before the 1980 Open at Muirfield, in the north of Scotland. I haven't talked about Jersey and my delight in victories at La Moye. Mid-Wales is an area unexplored for me, and so are King's Lynn, Sheringham, Royal Worlington and Woodhall Spa.

So much to be seen, and to do. Maybe the BBC will take the Alliss travels to these courses, which are acknowledged by all who know them as being among the finest in the land.

But always one remembers the old hunting grounds, the courses and the people with whom one shared the experiences of victory, defeats, good times, and not so good. I hope it goes on for many years yet.

6
In Conclusion: The Ryder Cup

People often ask what it is like to be a professional, and live a life on the golf tour. In this final chapter let me give an insight into those days when I lived from a suitcase and regarded it as an adventure. I'd also like to talk about Ryder Cup matches which have, I suppose, had a great bearing on my life.

Golf followers sometimes ask what I might have done if I had chosen not to follow in my father's footsteps. The answer is very straightforward . . . I have no idea!

As a young man I found that going into golf after National Service was the obvious thing to do. To begin with I did not boast a fast car, and always considered those with big cars really had made it. My golf chums and I joined up because we liked the idea of competing. Bernard Hunt and myself somehow grew up together, although we competed against each other and were rivals. We were of the same age, and our backgrounds were very similar, being sons of golf professionals.

But I teamed up with older players too. Dai Rees, Arthur Lees and Ken Bousfield were senior to me, but I joined them in practice rounds and learned from them and there were many more — John Jacobs, Dave Thomas and John Panton in particular. Maybe I joined a clique on the tour, but I wasn't conscious of it at the time. The press came along and by and large wrote kindly about a game which was business to us, and very much business to them. We all lived in each other's pockets, cars broke down and hotels turned out to be good, bad and ugly.

We had laughs, and made good friends. Today I'm lucky to be still involved with golf, thanks to television which has meant friends from years ago are often seen again, and new ones made. Maybe the younger tournament player today doesn't appreciate how lucky he is, and the rewards for his play are greater than some think he deserves. But most big winners have worked hard to gain their skill and I would be the last person in the world to begrudge them their fortunes, earned not only from the

(*left*) John Panton, a master of iron play (*Bert Neale*); (*right*) Guy Wolstenholme, looking very 'modern' for the year — 1961 (*Sport & General*)

prize money, but from the much greater endorsements available these days than back in the 1950s, when I was setting out on the trail. Then only the few, the very few, made big money from their talents. True, in the 1920s and 1930s Walter Hagen had shown there was money to be made and a little later the pre-eminence of Henry Cotton on the British scene had meant, for instance, that he topped the bill at the Colliseum in London, demonstrating his golf magicianship. But the top playing pros, only a rung below Henry in playing ability, were much further below him financially. Far more than today, they depended for a livelihood on the security of their club jobs, on selling, making and repairing clubs, studding golf shoes and giving lessons. Tournament winnings, when they came, were the jam on sparingly buttered bread; there might also be endorsement fees for the big names. Things remained much the same until the young Arnold Palmer swept round Cherry Hills, Denver, in 65 to take the 1960 US Open and a young lawyer called Mark McCormack saw that here was a personality that could be marketed; the major departure lay in the fact that he realised that the Palmer name could be used to sell and promote products quite outside the normal range of golf. The gold has since rubbed off on all the top players so that for years now we have been able to say that a win in the US or British Opens and the US Masters is 'worth a million' to the lucky man.

Golf has been kind to me in more ways than earnings and travel alone. If I had decided on some other career I might never have met such brilliant conversationalists as Henry Longhurst, or come across the sharp intellect of Henry Cotton or the characters who have ranged from caddies such as Little Mac, to the piano-playing wit of Guy Wolstenholme or the outspoken fun one has had with Christy O'Connor, Dai Rees or dear old Charles Roe.

You can look back on a tournament career in two or three ways. You can say it's a pity so-and-so didn't win the British Open, or you can argue about a contribution to a game which maybe, to some, is insignificant, concerning itself with the banging about of a ball. In the late evening, over brandy, you can play-act the cynic or you can end the evening chuckling, and remembering happy times. This, for me, is the way I look back and I thank God that, unlike so many other tournament golfers, I have not had to say farewell to the sport, because TV, the big jet and the motor car have meant I continue to roll round a circuit of people almost without comparison.

And all this, in an age when values are diminishing, some people muck-throwing and even the nicest people find less and less time to take part in the worthwhile things, be they fishing, talking, or playing golf on their favourite local course, with people they like.

Don't ask me to put a value on the game of golf, and don't ask me to say how much you should spend, or how much a new golf ball should cost because I know that, at the end of a day's golf with chums, in the right circumstances, people let down their hair and exchange stories and experiences — this is what makes golf such a classic pastime, without a price on it.

I look back some years because, maybe, I got into the business sooner than most. The big occasion has always thrilled me and there is not much bigger, for a British professional, than clashes with America in the Ryder Cup. Only playing the last nine holes in an Open championship, and ending the winner, is bigger. But slipping into the special blazer or pullover and to play for Britain against old Uncle Sam are peaks in my career.

So, for me, the Ryder Cup is really worth preserving. You might take the view that it's a pity we can't give the US a better fight and I admit to regretting that, somehow, over the years we didn't include the Commonwealth — preferring to include the Continent of Europe, which has virtually amalgamated with our own British PGA.

Craig Wood, who still holds the record for the longest measured drive in a tournament when he drove into a bunker 430 yards from the 5th tee during the 1933 Open at St Andrews. However, the ground was bone hard and there was a strong following wind

Of course this all makes sense because of the amalgamation and even the Common Market and so on, but it has crossed my mind how unlikely it is, if Britain and Eire had inflicted more defeats on the Americans, that they would have called for aid from Mexico — other than Lee Trevino — or appealed to South America and golfers in, say, Cuba or the Klondike!

I suppose my love, and that's what it has been, for the Ryder Cup stems from the fact that my father and I are the only father and son combination to have represented Britain in these matches. His record, despite missing out twice because he worked abroad, was pretty impressive and I feel good about that.

In 1933 he and Charles Whitcombe halved with the mighty Gene Sarazen and Walter Hagen and you can imagine just how the newspapers and public responded to that. And father went on to beat Paul Runyan 2 and 1.

Dad didn't always win. Two years later he and Alf Padgham were soundly walloped in the foursomes at Ridgewood, New Jersey, but he managed to score the only point for his side in the singles by beating Craig Wood by one hole, in a heatwave, with water poured over them at the 9th.

At Southport and Ainsdale in 1937 Father Alliss and Dick Burton, of the

The 1953 US Ryder Cup team. They are (back row left to right) Jim Turnesa, Walter Burkemo, Fred Haas, Dale Douglas, Ed Oliver, and Ted Kroll; (front row) Cary Middlecoff, Lloyd Mangrum, Sam Snead and Jack Burke (*Bert Neale*)

easy-swinging pitch shot, were winners 2 and 1 and in the singles clash he had a memorable battle with Sarazen where he was maddened by stymies and ricochets off the crowd to lose by the finest possible margin of 1 hole. And that was that. Hitler had arrived and there were no more matches for Alliss Senior.

I enjoy his scrapbook, thumbing through the photos. I used to do this as a youngster. So, in 1949, you can understand my excitement when word went around that young Alliss was considered a Ryder Cup possible. They reckoned I should be 'blooded' at Ganton against the US side which was to be led by Ben Hogan, who, recovering slowly from a dreadful road accident, was non-playing captain. The feeling was that we had little to lose as the previous match had ended in America slamming us.

As it turned out, caution prevailed. At 18 they probably thought Alliss too young and anyway I was doing National Service at the time. But the idea of playing for Britain certainly excited me, so in 1953, when they chose me for my first match, you can imagine how I felt.

Henry Cotton was captain and fussed around, making sure we were fed on steaks, despite the austerity which still prevailed in Britain eight years after the war. Cotton got us fixed up in posh digs opposite Sunningdale clubhouse in the old dormy house and I well recall the newspaper headlines, the billboards which screamed that Cotton was kicking his side into maximum effort and the general ballyhoo had to be heard and seen to be believed.

And, as I said earlier, it would have been nice to have won this one. It had been twenty years, almost to the day, since my father had been on the winning team at Southport and Ainsdale where the secretary there, in those days Captain Gerald Openshaw, had been so thrilled at our success that tears had appeared in his eyes.

Anyway I remember my shaking limbs and my jumping tummy as I stood on the 1st tee at Wentworth, partnering Harry Weetman against Dale Douglas and Ed 'Porky' Oliver. I held my end up in that clash, but a couple of whopping putts from Oliver and two strange shots from my partner at vital moments cost us that foursomes by 2 and 1.

But, as you probably know, it was in the singles that I had what the golf writers might describe as my worst moment in sport. I was one up and three to play against left-hander Jim Turnesa and he seemed to be headed for that delightful house off the 16th fairway in the woods and, as the ball flew, I confess that my spirits flew with it. But, woe was me, his ball got caught up in the crowd and stopped short of the out-of-bounds. Anyway, I was safely up the fairway and, as I say, in the lead. He knocked it out of trouble, some sixty yards up. I had a simple eight-iron to the green and it lay in longish grass.

Then came disaster. I lifted my head, just as I've told you not to do, hit the ground a bit 'fat' as the Americans say and although the shot looked reasonable, I knew it hadn't enough steam. Sure enough, it fell short into a bunker.

While Turnesa, no doubt encouraged by the sight, hit his third shot to ten feet. But wait a moment. All was not lost. I came out to within five feet. Then it happened. He holed and I did not. So we were square and spectators seemed to be rushing about demented.

On to the 17th tee, and I went straight out of bounds. With my second ball I could not get a four — so, obviously, he won the hole and took the lead. But at the final hole, Turnesa hit his ball into trees and now it was my turn to be encouraged. I hit it down the middle. He hacked it out of the

Peter Mills, who won his singles in the 1957 Ryder Cup (*Bert Neale*)

jungle — it was thick in those days — and his third shot at this long par-5 hole was still thirty yards short of the green. My second was dragged a bit left of the green, and after he had pitched his fourth stroke to within about fifteen feet of the flag, I was faced with a nasty little pitch up the slope.

I recall to this day looking at my ball, which lay in a mossy-looking lie. As I lined up a huge silence fell, and suddenly I could see the feet of the people sitting in the stands. They were there, clearly in the corner of my eye.

One highly polished pair of brown brogues stick in my memory. They belonged to Col Tony Duncan, the very good amateur from Wales. I don't know if it was the shine on his shoes or my fluttering nerves but I took a sand iron and again hit the ground a little heavy and left the ball just on the edge of the green. A good chip to within three feet followed, Turnesa missed his putt and now I had one to halve the match but, of course, I didn't get within inches.

A great groan went up, to be followed by another groan ten minutes later when Bernard Hunt three-putted from the back of the green to only halve his match, when two putts would have been good enough.

We both got severely pulled over the coals for that and, in fact, in 1955 although I had the best two rounds — 68s — in the Dunlop Masters at Little Aston, I also had two 74s and was dropped from the team. I remember that night well. I had too many drinks and spent the time blubbering away and behaving like a spoilt lad.

Along came 1957 and I was paired with Bernard Hunt in the foursomes. I remember we played steadily without holing too many putts and were beaten 2 and 1 by Doug Ford and Dow Finsterwald. We were losing 3-1 in the foursomes and then in the singles all hell seemed to break loose. As almost all our men got two up, then three up, cheers rang out around the course. Harry Bradshaw halved, everyone else won and Peter Alliss was the only loser. So, in the midst of great elation there was sadness for me because I had again failed to score a point.

It wasn't in fact, until 1959 that I began my long and marvellous association with the great Irish player Christy O'Connor. Neither of us at that time were renowned for our putting and we were drawn in the foursomes against Doug Ford and Art Wall, two of the greatest exponents the world has ever seen of the devilish side of golf. They couldn't really believe it when we beat them 3 and 2. We played 36 holes in those days and it was, indeed, a long hot day. I managed to halve my singles with Jay Herbert, who at the time was US PGA champion, and, although we lost the match 7-2 with three halves, I was beginning to feel better.

My association with Christy went on for several years and we were a pretty hard combination to beat. We managed to get some good scalps. It was in 1961, though, when Arnold Palmer was at the height of his fame and the fortunes of British Open were being revived that I took on the mighty man. The format had already been changed to 18-hole matches and so, having won one and lost one with O'Connor, I found myself up against Palmer.

That day he holed out from off the green on no fewer than three occasions. The first was a chip-in on the par-5 7th; then there was another chip-in from over the back of the 10th, followed by a holed bunker shot from the side of the 15th green. I was not at all pleased. I shall never forget the words of that great writer, character and golfer Leonard Crawley in one of his pieces. He said: 'When Palmer's ball went in the hole at the 15th, Alliss's face remained completely expressionless. If I had to choose anyone to play poker for my life it would, indeed, be this young man.'

Standing on the 18th we were all square. I drove into the rough to the left-hand side of the fairway. Palmer hit a real fizzer. I couldn't reach the green in two, but managed to get in the middle, some fifteen yards short. Palmer hit his second right at the flag, but it bit into the green quickly, and stopped eighteen feet short.

I remember thinking: here we go again. I've played well, he's holed out three times from off the green and I'm going to be beaten one up. I walked on to the green and looked up at those big windows that stare down from the clubhouse some 15 feet behind the 18th green and there, sitting in the middle right-hand window, was my father looking down. He gave me the thumbs-up. Well, I don't know quite what he meant by the thumbs-up sign but I went back. I knew I'd played plenty of good chip and runs. Out came the faithful 9-iron; hands forward, slow back, I tried to remember all those hours of coaching from Ken Bousfield on the art of delicate chipping. My ball tumbled along and I knew it was good. It kept going and eventually finished some two feet from the hole.

Palmer walked up slowly; I walked up even slower. 'Mark it', he said. He then went through his familiar routine, looked up at the hole and said 'I'll give you that'. Quick as a flash, before he had time to change his mind, I was over and picked up my coin marker. He then had a real run at his and put it some two feet past. He walked up, looked over his short putt, took his stance and then I thought we had had a great match. I was delighted with the way it was going to end and said 'I'll give you that one, Arnold.' I will never forget the look on his face. That rather crooked grin appeared, and we shook hands.

Two years later, we were over at Atlanta, Georgia, and I found myself drawn against the great man once again, and this time in his natural habitat.

(*left*) Palmer follows an approach shot anxiously (*Peter Dazeley Photography*); (*right*) Christy O'Connor: no finer striker ever (*Bert Neale*)

I had been driving badly and was reduced to a 3-wood off the tee. So Palmer was out-driving me by 40 or 50 yards. Anyway, we managed to get to the 17th hole with me 1 up. I put my second shot fifteen feet from the hole; Palmer put his three feet away and the locals were screaming. 'Go get him Arnie. Kill him, smash him, destroy him.' I'm sure they didn't really mean it but I did get a feeling of being thrown to the lions!

How it happened I don't know but my fifteen-footer went straight into the middle of the hole. Suddenly, Palmer was faced with a tricky little three-footer to avoid defeat by 2 and 1. Well, he holed it. At the 18th, a long short hole across a valley to an elevated green, I hit a 2-iron, which finished on the right-hand side of the green, leaving a huge, sloping putt of about twenty-five yards with a borrow of about eight feet. Palmer smashed his right at the hole. His ball, instead of getting backspin, bounced forward and ended up some twenty feet past the hole. I tried not to think negatively and got down to the business of putting mine close. It actually touched the hole from that distance and nestled five or six inches away, on the top side, giving Palmer almost a complete stymie. It was conceded and he settled over his ball. I had no doubt in my mind he would hole it but on this occasion he hit it far too firmly and missed by at least eighteen inches on the right and went yards past. I had won.

What jubilation, but not too much time for celebration, for in the afternoon I was out again in match three against Tony Lema. A half this time and I was the only one in our team not to lose, although there were some marvellous battles. But the end result, United States 20, Great Britain 6 with 6 halves — looked pretty miserable.

In 1965 I continued my association with Christy at Royal Birkdale. In the foursomes, we were almost invincible, winning one far from home and the other comfortably. At the end of the foursomes, it was level at 4-4.

Unhappily, in the four-balls, it was a different story. Arnold Palmer and Dave Marr had their revenge on us, winning by a clear margin and in the afternoon, as luck had it, we again drew this formidable pair. But this time we managed to turn the tide, and beat them — but only just. Actually, at the 18th hole I played one of the few shots of my career I can honestly say I clearly remember. We were one up and Arnold had put his shot into the bunker to the right of the green. Marr was thirty yards short, Christy was away in sand and I had hit the longest drive. I noticed the slight breeze, from the right and as I only carried two woods in those days, I had to go with the 4-wood. I recalled a tip John Jacobs had given me. Close in the toe of this club, keep the hands just a fraction ahead and drill the ball down the right hand side of the fairway. So this was my plan of attack, and it came off perfectly.

In my entire competitive life, I don't think I've ever hit a better shot. It did as I had bid, pitching some fifteen yards short of the green and rolling on with the slight hook to within ten feet of the hole. But it wasn't over yet. Marr's chip, I'll swear, touched the edge of the hole. Palmer's bunker shot wasn't too good and I remember thinking I could get down in two from ten feet no matter what happened. So what did happen? Amazingly I wasn't even asked to putt. With good grace, they surrendered and Marr, talking with golf writer John Ingham later, said: 'I hope that baby [Alliss] doesn't come and play the US tour.'

So the four-balls ended and we were trailing 8-6 with all the singles to come. I eased out Billy Casper by one hole, knocking in a frightful last green putt after discovering the ball was actually in either a pitch mark, or a poor spot. Friends groaned as I examined the spot. But after a pause, I knocked it straight into the hole without a tremor.

(*left*) A golfer whose swing has lasted well. Winner of the 1961 US Open, Gene Littler is still making money on the US tour and almost won the US PGA in 1977, losing in a play-off to Lanny Wadkins (*Peter Dazeley Photography*); (*right*) Doug Sanders, and, believe it or not, he's about at the 'top' of his backswing (*Peter Dazeley Photography*)

In the afternoon I managed to beat Ken Venturi, the United States Open champion that year, by 3 and 1 and I'd gone through the series, helped by old pal Christy, and lost only one match to score five points out of six with rounds in the 60s. And I'll admit now that I groaned to a chum as I pulled off my spiked shoes. And my groan was that if I had reproduced the kind of winning Ryder Cup form in the Open at Birkdale, then nobody would have stopped me. What a big word it is, 'if'!

In 1967 the matches were held at Houston and the Allis-O'Connor partnership lost twice in the foursomes. And we lost the first of the four-balls and then, in the afternoon the captain decided he would ring the changes so Dai Rees put me out with Malcolm Gregson. But the result was a 3 and 2 defeat at the hands of Gardner Dickinson and short-swinging Doug Sanders. In the singles, Casper had his revenge on me and things looked bleak. In the afternoon I faced Gay Brewer, holder of the Masters and a man with a most interesting loop to his swing. My putting was beginning to shake but, despite this, I managed to beat him.

So it was back to Royal Birkdale in 1969 and, to be perfectly frank, the writing was beginning to appear on the locker-room wall as far as my career was concerned. Although Christy and I managed to halve with Casper and Frank Beard, my putting was beginning to jerk and heave. As Henry Longhurst used to say: 'If you've got 'em, you've got 'em!' and I seemed to have the occasional twitch.

Even Christy was beginning to tire, so they made me play with Brian Barnes in the first of the four-balls. We were beaten by one hole, going down to Lee Trevino and Gene Littler, later to suffer from cancer, and then beat it so wonderfully. In the top singles I lost to Trevino by 2 and 1 and at the end of the day it was a halved Ryder Cup!

At the end of 1969 I announced, to anyone who cared to listen, that I considered my team days over and I can truthfully look back and say that making that decision was one of the biggest disappointments of my life. Cup matches, you see, had given me some of the proudest moments. You can recall Brian Huggett knocking in a putt on the 18th green, thinking that putt had clinched the match and we all know how he was overcome with emotion. And you cannot dismiss the Jacklin *v* Nicklaus halved clash with Jack conceding a putt that many would have required to be knocked in.

The matches go on, and many changes have occurred. I still favour the system of team selection, but folk will complain that the selectors would/could have favourites, or are motivated by the wrong reason.

They've tried points, money and almost every other system except calling in the witch doctor. I feel that a few players are far better at match-play than they are at the four-round stroke-play game — and vice versa. Nicklaus, for

I represented England in the Canada Cup (now the World Cup) on 10 occasions.
Here I'm in Hawaii for the 1964 event with Bernard Hunt and Ernest Butten

instance, has by no means a great Ryder Cup record, while Peter Oosterhuis has. Eric Brown, in the 1950s seemed to thrive on match-play. Personally I should go for picking the men in form, especially if I felt they would thrive on the head-to-head encounter. Though in all conscience it would be difficult indeed to judge this nowadays, with the scarcity of match-play events for professionals. Perhaps anyway the truth is we are always a little short of top players and, even with Europe now included, bottom of the team is usually on the weak side so that if somebody falls ill, we don't have the strength in depth that America has, being able to draw on the cream of 15 million golfers!

What does annoy me is the apparent disregard some players have for the honour of representing their country. Americans, as a rule, regard playing for their nation as important. Whom they play against isn't greatly important, but playing for the flag matters and I too take this view and am old fashioned enough to say so.

Those British pros who think the honour small beer impress me not at all, particularly as they usually include the fact that they are Ryder Cup men on their headed note paper. And whenever they apply for a job, one of the first things they boast about is playing for their country.

There are a lot of things I'd like to see changed. I find it distressing to see bad behaviour from pro golfers and am proud that these outbursts are rare. If a Ryder Cup man steps out of line then what else can you do but fine him? Slapping his wrist is pointless.

But golf, interestingly, tends to breed good behaviour in people. We put on a clean sports shirt, we buy the other fellow a drink and say 'Well played' if he hits a good shot. And at the end of a round, on the pro circuit, the chaps shake hands and thank each other. You may argue it's all superficial and at heart they are as ruthless as any sportsman. All right — but at least an example is being set to youngsters, and golf can do it. And it's not such a bad thing, either.

Index

230